Memoirs of an Ancient Lady

Memoirs of an Ancient Lady

by

Jessica Godwin

The Pentland Press Limited
Edinburgh · Cambridge · Durham

First Published in 1992 by
The Pentland Press Ltd.
Brockerscliffe
Witton le Wear
Durham

ISBN 1 872795 64 1

Typeset by Elite Typesetting Techniques
Southampton.
Printed and bound by Antony Rowe Ltd.,
Chippenham.
Jacket design by Geoff Hobbs

Acknowledgement

William Bloomfield Esq., for his help, support and encouragement.

Foreword

On a sunny afternoon in the 1980s I first met Jessica Godwin walking in Green Park, Bath. She told me she was going to Canada to visit her relatives, 'and then she thought she might pop over to Australia to see a friend she had not seen for forty years'. She said that she was travelling by plane, and I asked her where the plane stopped *en route* from Australia and back to England. She said, 'I really don't know, dear, I leave it to the pilots; you see, they know what to do'. They asked her up onto the Flight Deck of the aircraft and Jessica thought the noise was rather louder than it should be – 'Could you switch something off,' she asked the captain.

Perhaps this typifies the whole attitude of the great lady who was ninety-six years of age at the time. Every Sunday she walks the half-mile to church, and always feeds the birds in Kingmead Square, quite close to her home.

When Jessica bought her present home in Green Park, Bath, she was eighty-nine years and the property was purchased by her for her life-time; it would then revert back to the previous owner, on her demise. At the age of ninety-nine, she met the previous owner and apologized to him for living so long!

This is the kind of special lady she is. Enjoy the book.

William Bloomfield

Preface

On 2 March 1992 I shall be one hundred years of age. Born in Worthing in 1892, my life has spanned ten decades – at the age of three I was placed in a home for the fatherless; at eight I worked in my mother's house, and learned the three Rs; when I was fourteen I became a companion/help to a lady in London; in the First World War I joined the Land Army and was driving tractors. Ploughing at Chequer's Court (now the country home of our Prime Minister), after the war, I married a farmer, and the late 1920s I purchased a Georgian house in Lansdown, Bath, and made it into apartments for gentleladies. In 1942, a bomb exploded in my garden taking the roof off.

I now live in a Georgian house in Green Park, Bath, next door to where Jane Austen once lived – having travelled the world, Bath is the most wonderful place to live.

wanted him to still live in the farmhouse, but Daisy, his bride, said no. She would be content with only two rooms, but share the farmhouse she would not. It vexed and annoyed my uncle so much that when he died he left Philip only $200 and my sister Annie came in for everything.

Philip was a gentle, studious man not fitted for rough farm life, although he worked conscientiously. I never saw him again after he went to Canada, but his son says he was the most Christlike man he has ever met and all his children adored him. How I wish I had known him, but I know and love very dearly his four daughters and his son.

Well, now my mother had disposed of her two sons. The two-day-old baby boy she said she would never part with, as he was a legacy from my father. The two eldest girls, Hettie and Annie, were put out to Service, that wonderful English Institution where girls went as soon as they left school at thirteen or fourteen years of age. They had no experience; they just knew what they had learned from their mothers. Sometimes they started as scullery maids in a large household, or as a maid-of-all-work in, usually, a trademan's household. We ourselves had had a little maid in the early married years. They were paid 2s.6d. a week and had one free half-day a week and every other Sunday – a terribly hard life.

Well, there was only me left to dispose of, so I was sent to 'Dr Toyes Home for the Fatherless'. It was at Blackheath Hill, Lewisham, London. I wonder how I got there? Perhaps my Uncle William took me on his way home with my brother Frank, as my uncle lived in London. However, when I got there I was told I would be called '85', but I think I must have been the youngest one there as they called me 'little 85'!

I was still a sickly child with weeping eczema. I had it at the back of my knees, inside the elbow joints and at my throat. They were very kind to us at the Home. We sickly ones were given a spoonful of cod liver oil and malt every morning, and when the jar was nearly empty they would say, 'Here, little 85, you sit on the step and lick out the jar!' I loved it and could get my hand right in the jar. I bet I licked it out 'as clean as a whistle'.

During the four and a half years I was at the Home I had no contact with any of my family. My mother may have enquired after me, but if she did I was not told. It is strange how little I can recall about the Home. I know we wore grey frocks and navy blue capes and a bonnet style of hat, and we would be taken for walks, but we had a large playground and had fun there with each other. One strict rule was that we ate everything we were given. Nothing was to be left on our plates. So if there was something one of us did not really like, there was always another girl who would willingly take it.

When I was eight years old I was called into the Matron's room and she told me that my mother had remarried and that I was being sent home and, said Matron, 'Look at the lovely clothes your mother has made for you!' To me they *were* lovely and all handmade.

I said, 'She must want me, to have made such nice clothes!'

'Why of course she wants you,' said Matron. 'You are a lucky girl to be going home to a mother and father!'

But I was miserable, as the Home was the only home I could remember. Matron sent for one of the girls to bath me and she herself dressed me in my new clothes. There was a calico chemise and drawers, as we called them, both trimmed with cotton embroidery; a liberty bodice, a thing I had never worn before; a cream flannel petticoat and a beautifully tucked white cotton one; and a navy blue cotton dress with white spots, white stockings and black boots; a little straw hat with a wreath of little flowers round it; a handkerchief and a pair of white cotton gloves. I felt like a princess, but I felt rather frightened at leaving the Home.

Matron said my aunt and a cousin would be coming to fetch me and put me on a train, and in a short while they arrived. I had never seen them before and I thought they were very grand. Matron kissed me goodbye and said, 'We are going to miss you, little 85.' I just quietly left. No fanfare!

We walked to London Bridge and it started to rain.

'Oh dear,' said my aunt in an annoyed tone of voice, 'how like Sally not to provide a coat for the child.'

So she took me into a shop – the first shop I had ever been into in my life! and bought me a grey coat with a fur collar. I expect it was rabbit, but I thought it was lovely and enjoyed stroking it. I was put on the train; the first train or, in fact, any conveyance I ever remember riding in!

Chapter 2

At Brighton Station my mother and stepfather were waiting on the platform, total strangers to me! My mother was a short lady, 4 ft. 11 in., and my stepfather was 6 ft. 2 in., a very handsome man, but of course I did not notice this then. All I knew was that my mother was short and my father very tall. My mother kissed me and said, 'We will walk home, it is not far.'

I had nothing to carry. Everything I possessed was on my body! – not a parting gift from anyone, but I did not worry about this then as I did not expect anything, or know anything about giving and receiving presents.

After a short walk we came to 14 John Street and I went in to the first *real* home I had known! The front door opened to a passage-type hall and we went into a sitting-room where tea was already laid.

'Come out into the kitchen with me,' said my mother, 'while I make the tea.'

The black kettle was already singing on a hob by the side of a cheerful fire in a range with a little oven at the side. She made the tea and we went back into the pretty little sitting-room. It did seem *very* little to me, as of course at the Home all the rooms were very large, but I thought it was lovely.

After we had finished tea my mother took me upstairs where there were two bedrooms. The one we were in had a curtain across a part of it. We went behind and there in a sort of cot was a very small boy fast asleep.

'This,' said my mother, 'is your little brother, Willie, and I hope you will love him and take great care of him. He is very precious to me.' She kissed me good-night and said she would call me in the morning.

'And when I do, you must get up and dress quickly and help Willie to dress and come down to breakfast which we will have in the kitchen. Then I must take you to your new school and see the headmistress.'

The headmistress was a little wizened woman wearing pince-nez. I did not like the look of her and she took an instant dislike to me. If, during the two years I was there, she could humiliate me, she did! I don't think there was another child there in such poor circumstances as those we were in.

While we were having breakfast my stepfather said, 'I got the sack yesterday.'

'Oh Jim,' said my mother in an exasperated voice, 'just as we have another mouth to feed.'

'I'm sorry mother,' I said, 'I'll try not to eat much.'

She just looked at me and said, 'Come along both of you or you'll be late for school.'

The little house was one in a row of identical ones. Half-way down the street was a bakery and there anyone who could afford a roast dinner, especially on a Sunday, would take it down to the bakery to be cooked. The only time I ever took anything down was when my father made a bread and butter pudding, but he had not put an egg in it, so that when it was cooked it was just bread and butter and a few currants swimming about in milk. I had a job to carry it without spilling it, especially as it was hot. I carried it on a small tin tray. When I got to the house, a couple of boys were sitting on the step. I asked them to move and they wouldn't, so I stepped over them and shot the pudding all over the mat inside the door. I got a terrible beating and I had to pick up the bread (which broke to pieces) and we had to eat it, dirt and all!

At the other end of the street was a large grocer's shop kept by Mr Barrett. His little daughter, Maggie, came to the same school as me, St John's School just round the corner. Maggie had lovely long ringlets and lovely clothes. I did envy her.

Across the road opposite our house was a second-hand clothes shop, kept by Mrs Wragg. She had two daughters, but they went to a different school, but we were great friends. Next was a fish and chip shop. This was in the year 1900, so fish and chips have been sold in England for a very long time. One could buy a tuppenny piece of fish and a haporth of chips, though I don't remember ever *buying* any, but I was given some to bring home, after I had minded the baby for them. At the corner was a public house, which was of no interest to us as even my stepfather was an abstainer and did not smoke or swear, but he did not like to work!

In our kitchen there was a copper and the fire was lit underneath when my mother did the washing and when we had baths. The 'loo' or privy, as it was called in those days, was at the end of the yard, and the tin bath was hung on a nail outside the back-door. I used to go to the carpenter's workshop with a sack which I stuffed full with shavings and bits of wood for the copper fire. The carpenter and his mate were only too glad for me to gather up the wood shavings, and it was a job I liked.

On Monday mornings I had to get up extra early and take a clean pillowcase to the very large baker's shop in town and join the queue for six pennyworth of stale bread. It was marvellous what a lot one got, and it was exciting to turn out the pillowcase and find cakes and rolls as well as bread. My mother would use the stalist to make a bread pudding. The fire in the kitchen was lit winter and summer, because that was the only way we had of boiling a kettle, or cooking a stew. We had no gas or electricity.

My mother was now going out to work each day. She could always get work. She was a good cook and really liked cooking, but she was resentful that she had to be the breadwinner. She would leave before Willie and I left for school. She would put some swede on the stove and tell me to mash it with some salt and pepper and put a layer on bread and butter (marg.) for dinner for Willie and me. When she cooked 'late' dinners it would be 8 o'clock before she got home, and Willie and I would be in bed.

For some reason, known only to God and my father, my father hated my little brother and he would beat him with or without provocation. We were always taken to the front door for a beating. Had he beaten us in the kitchen, the neighbours could have heard us screaming. He would take off his belt and the buckle end would come across our backs. He only meant to beat Willie, but I would cry, so he would give me something to cry about! We were so frightened, we would both wet ourselves, and then we were called 'dirty little tykes'. Willie was only five years old and such a little boy! We never told my mother – we were afraid to!

One evening she came home a bit earlier and we were not in bed. She looked at us and said, 'You poor neglected looking little miseries. What you need is a good bath and some clean clothes. There is not time to light the copper so I'll make do with kettles of hot water in the big bowl. Come Willie, I'll do you first because it is already past your bedtime.'

She undressed him and when she saw the weals on his back she went for me like a tigress.

'Why have you not taken better care of him?'

'I'm sorry mother,' I said, 'but he beats me too'.

She did not speak again while she carefully washed Willie. Then she took him in her arms and said, 'Put some more water in the bowl and wash yourself all over. I will come to you when I have put Willie to bed.'

As she went upstairs I heard her say, 'My poor baby. My poor little darling boy,' and she was crying.

When she came down she looked at my back and put some vaseline on it. She said, 'I'm sorry I was so sharp with you. This won't happen again, as I shall take Willie to the Inspector for the NSPCC tomorrow and he will come and talk to your father.'

It was a month or two before we were beaten again and I told my mother, as she had made me promise to do so. The result was that she put Willie into Dr Barnardo's Home. She said it was for his own protection, but it upset her very much as I am sure that Willie was the only child she truly loved.

When he was nine years old he was sent out to Canada, and that nearly broke my mother's heart. From that day her secret ambition was to get to Canada and make a home for her three sons. When Willie went into the Home he was nearly six years old and I never saw him again until he came over to England in the First World War. He was twenty years old but in Canada one had to have the consent of one's parents before one could join up, if one was under twenty-one. As my mother would not give her consent, he came over and joined up here for – was it really only a shilling a day? He went right through the war without even being wounded and ended up as a Sergeant.

Once my brother was gone, my father was very nice to me. He could not seem to do enough for me, to show his affection. My mother naturally felt very bitter towards him and so did my sister Annie, though she did not know him. I never even remember her coming to visit us, although she only lived in Croydon, so she had no means of getting to know him. But from the time Willie left at six years old and I was nine, I lived with him until I was fourteen and he never said a wrong word to me. When I read today of fathers and stepfathers molesting their daughters, I realize that he must have been a decent man. Sometimes we only had one room, and my mother would have gone to work, and I would get up and dress in front of my father with absolute innocence.

He used to mend my boots and would hand sew the soles on, because he wasn't going to have the nails hurt my little feet! Alas, he did not know the right way to mend them and in a few days the stitches would be worn through and my soles would be going flip-flop. I would tell my mother my soles were coming off and she would say, 'Don't tell your father. I will sew them on for you,' And she would run the string through some beeswax, and using the same holes my father had made, she would sew them on again.

My father was a very clean man. He had a bald head in places and he used to buy 'Edwards Harlone Hair Tonic', I think it was called, and put a little in his hands and rub it all over his head. Mother used to be furious, 'Spending money on that stuff when we have not enough to eat.'

The funny thing was, *he* always seemed to have money. If I asked him for a penny he would bring out a handful of money, silver and coppers, and say, 'Don't tell your mother you saw that.'

I wonder now if he used to bet. I once saw him in the corner public house and ran home to tell my mother. She said, 'Forget it, and stop telling tales.'

When my father worked he did all sorts of jobs. Sometimes he would be a sandwich man, carrying two boards, one in front and one at the back, to advertise something. Sometimes he would take his shoe box out, and sometimes he would be a nightwatchman, sitting by a coke brazier minding a hole in the road! When he did this, I have known my mother to take out a can of hot tea and some sandwiches at 12 o'clock at night and sit and chat with him for a while to encourage him to keep the job, because he never held down a job for more than a few weeks. When he was working, my mother would stay at home and do sewing. She made beautiful underwear and I would sit and help her in any way I could. When a job was done, she would get me to take it to the lady and she would say, 'Don't ask for the money, but if she says, "Does your mother want the money tonight?" say yes please.'

So I would take it. It might be as late as 9 o'clock (but in those days we never knew anything about muggings or little girls, or boys, being molested) and I would wait while Mrs Cuthbert looked at it and she would say, 'How beautifully your mother sews.'

And I would say, 'Did she put in how much it was?'

And she would say, 'Why yes. Does your mother want the money tonight?'

And I would say, 'Oh yes please,' and run home joyfully with the money clasped in my little hot hand.

'Did you get the money?' my mother would ask, and when I gave it to her she would say, 'Thank God. Tomorrow I will buy us some food!'

One day my friend Elsie Thomas said they were going out on May Day to sing and collect money, and if I had a white or light coloured dress, I could go with them. My mother fixed me up with a frock and on May 1st I ran round to the Thomas's. Mrs Thomas had decorated two hoops with garlands of flowers and greenery, and each of us eight girls had a wreath of flowers round our heads. Away we went with a large cocoa tin with a slit in the lid. We went to the part of the town where there were big houses and we formed a ring and sang, or rather recited first,

> 'Please remember the First of May,
> It is the ladies' garland day,
> Say what you will, say what you may,
> But please remember the First of May.'

And then we would sing,

> 'All in the sunlight
> Underneath the trees
> There you may find her
> Tell her what you please.
> Tell that you love her
> On your bended knee
> All in the sunlight
> Underneath the tree.'

And we would do the actions, with one girl going down on her knee and taking the hand of the other girl and gazing at each other most soulfully. One of us would ring the door bells and rattle our money tin. It sounds daft to me now, but I think we made a pretty sight and our young voices were very sweet. At 1 o'clock we went back to Mrs Thomas and she gave us lemonade and a piece of cake and freshened up our garlands, and away we went again until soon after 4 o'clock. Not one of us had a watch; we guessed when it was about four and we had heard the 1 o'clock hooter. When we got back to Mrs Thomas, she emptied our cocoa tin and shared the money out equally. We had one shilling and fourpence each and we had enjoyed ourselves very much. I could not run home fast enough and give the money to my mother. She was so pleased and sent me back to say a special thank-you to Mrs Thomas and her two girls.

The summer passed pleasantly, although I was not allowed to skip or play hopscotch as it would wear out my boots! I did have a hoop and a ball and also a wooden top, which I used to whip along the pavement, and got quite expert at.

Chapter 3

One morning early in September my mother woke me up. She said it was 5 o'clock! I asked her why she was up and dressed so early. She said we were going hop-picking way out in the country and that we would have to walk there as we had no money for train fares. When I got downstairs my father was stuffing things into a big sack and my mother was pushing things into two smaller ones. I did not know what 'going hop-picking' meant and she said she would tell me all about it as we went, but now I must eat my breakfast quickly as she was anxious to leave the house before the neighbours were about. So by 5.30 we were ready to start.

When we got to Preston Park district, my mother told my father and me to wait while she ran up to my sister Hettie's house to tell her we were going. My sister was now married and living in a very nice house. Her husband was twelve years her senior, which made him twenty-four years older than me, so I was to address him as Mr Tom. My mother thought it dreadful for a child to address a man his age by his Christian name without a prefix! Well I suppose my mother had a job to rouse Hettie so early on a Sunday morning as she was a long time gone.

'Look,' said my father, 'I am not going to wait any longer. Will you come with me or wait for your mother?'

'Oh I will wait for my mother.'

So off he went and I waited.

'Where is your father?' asked my mother on returning.

'He said he wouldn't wait any longer, so has gone on.'

'Never mind,' said my mother, 'we will soon catch him up.'

This made me laugh because when they went out together my mother had to keep doing little running steps to keep up with him for he was so tall and had such a long stride. We picked up our bundles and went merrily on.

When we reached Lewis and came to a large dreary building, I asked my mother what it was and she said it was a prison and, 'That, my dear, is one place we shall *never* enter.'

By nightfall we had reached the country and we had not seen anything of my father. My mother found a field with ricks in it and she told me to snuggle down and get some sleep.

'Are you not sleeping too?' I asked.

She said, 'I must keep watch.'

'Whatever for?'

'Well, if a policeman saw us he might take us up as vagrants, and *that* I could not bear! I will wake you in two or three hours and then you must watch.'

We had brought all the food, mostly bread, from home and I was told to keep a look out for a stream so that we could drink and wash. My mother was very particular about cleanliness.

About 12.30 next day we met a man. He stopped and looked us up and down and said, 'Missus, I met your bloke and he said if I see you I were to tell 'ee to hurry up!'

'What time was that?' asked my mother.

'Oh, 'twas about 8 o'clock this morning.'

'Then I'm afraid we won't catch him up,' said my mother, 'but thank you for the message.'

We walked on but had great difficulty in reading the signposts as they were very tall in those days. I notice now they are much more accessible. Our bundles got very heavy and I got very hungry. My mother avoided a village as much as possible. Once when we passed a cottage garden with a lot of fallen apples on the grass, my mother told me to go and ask the lady if she would sell me a halfpenny worth? The lady smiled and said, 'Keep your money and pick up as many as you can carry in your pinny,' which I did.

About 4 o'clock we saw written in the gravel: PASSED HERE AT 12 O'CLOCK, JIM.

'Oh good,' said mother, 'we are on the right road.'

When I was dozing by a hayrick that night, my mother suddenly rushed to me and flopped down saying,

'Oh dear! Oh dear!'

'Whatever is the matter, mother?'

'There is a drunken man in the lane, and a drunken man is the only thing I am afraid of,' she said.

I went and looked and there was a lone cow grazing by the grass verge! In 1900 there were no lights in the country lanes and villages.

I can't remember what we did for food as I know we did not once go into a village shop. We tried to go through the villages when it was dark, as my mother did not want people to see us and think we were tramps.

'I want,' said my mother, 'for us to reach Tunbridge Wells by Thursday morning, as the farmer is sending a wagon to meet the people from the East End of London off the train and give them a ride for the seven miles to the farm, and if we are there we are sure to get a ride.'

So we got into Tunbridge Wells at about 5 o'clock and my mother said, 'My nose tells me we are near a bakery.'

So we followed our noses and sure enough there was the baker and his man making loaves. The door was open and my mother knocked gently and said, 'Good morning, I wonder if you would kindly sell me a loaf. My little girl and I have been walking since Sunday and have had very little to eat.'

'Where have you come from?' asked the baker.

'From Brighton.'

'Bless my soul! You and the little un have walked all the way from Brighton? Here, come you in and sit down. My missus will be down soon to make us our breakfast and you shall share it with us!'

'No indeed,' said my mother, 'that is most kind of you but I'll just buy the loaf and we will be on our way as we must be at the station by 8 o'clock,' and she explained why.

'Now don't you worry,' said the baker; 'you will have plenty of time to eat your breakfast, and here's my missus!' and he told her our story.

She said, 'You poor brave souls. You shall share with us,' and she gave us egg and bacon and tea, the first hot drink we had had since we left home on Sunday. Oh it was good and the first time I had ever had eggs and bacon together. We were given some rolls to bring away and they would not take a penny from us.

We made our way to the station feeling much better for the food and tea. When my mother saw the wagon belonging to the farmer we were going to work for (his name was on the side), she went up to the driver and told him we were going to pick hops for his boss and could we have a lift for the last seven miles as we had walked from Brighton?

'No, missus,' said the man, 'I can't do that. I was told to pick up the East-Enders off the train and you won't be coming off the train!'

'No, I know,' said my mother, 'but I'm sure your boss would want you to give us a ride.'

'I can't do that,' said the stupid man. 'I were told to pick up the people off the train, not no one else.'

So we walked the last seven miles, and they were the longest. My mother was a very cheerful person, but that really did seem to depress her.

We got to the hop field. The East-Enders had already arrived and were fixing themselves up for a stay of six weeks. As far as I remember, each family had a hut and there were tripods on which one could hang a kettle or a pot. I think we were allowed the first day to settle in but had to be up early the next morning to start at 7 o'clock.

My mother and I wandered around looking for my stepfather and never saw him. The East-Enders were most kind to us. They said it was a bloody shame that we had had to walk the last seven miles and, 'Now you can't find your old man. Never mind me ducks, you come and have a bite of our grub,' and they made us share their very good stew.

My mother said we could not possibly stay without the things my father carried in his packs, so we walked back to Tunbridge Wells and I felt very poorly. I told my mother and she looked at me and felt my forehead, and said, 'You certainly are not well. We had better go to the Workhouse and ask for a night's lodgings.'

Of course having been in the Home until I was eight years old, I knew nothing about workhouses. However, we made our way to it and explained to the two ladies in charge what had happened, and they looked at me and said, 'Yes, definitely she is not well,' and showed where we were to sleep.

It was a barn like place with straw matresses on the floor and brown blankets to cover us. There were already several women sleeping, or if they were awake they did not speak to us and we did not speak to them. We laid down as we were, in our clothes, and had a very restless night. We must have dropped off towards morning for when we woke the place was empty. So we went out to the wash-basins and had a good, much needed wash and then went to the office to see the ladies. When one gets a night's lodgings in a casual ward one is supposed to do a day's work to pay for it. The ladies said they did not think either of us were fit to walk back to Brighton so they were going to put us on the train as soon as we had had some breakfast, which was porridge, bread and margarine, and tea.

As soon as we got home my mother put me to bed and said she must just run to tell Hettie what had happened and that we were home again. To get to Preston Park district must be more than a mile from where we lived, so it was an hour or more before my mother returned with Hettie.

Hettie was always fond of me. Now she said, 'Little tuppenny, what have you been up to, getting poorly like this? Is there anything you want?'

'Yes,' I said, 'I would like an orange.'

'I'll see if I can get one, but you know we don't usually see them until Christmas.'

She was a long time gone, but she came back with an orange.

'Jess,' she said, 'it was awfully dear. I had to pay threepence for it!' That was indeed a lot in those days, and at Christmas time, when there were plenty in the shops, they were as little as two a penny!

I don't know what was the matter with me, but I was in bed for a couple of weeks. My mother had to leave me to go out to work, but Hettie came each day and I loved having her. She petted me, a thing my mother never did.

At the end of six weeks my father came home. He had gone to the wrong farmer but of course was given hop-picking to do. My mother was very vexed with him and did not think he had earned enough money.

We went hop-picking the two following years, walking both ways each time, and I loved every minute of it. I was fascinated by the glow-worms in the hedgerows. I never see them nowadays.

Chapter 4

I was now twelve years old and my mother said, 'Jessie, I am tired of keeping Jim Tribe and I have seen Mrs Cohen at the Renata Hotel and have arranged to go and work for her. You are to come as well and we will live at the hotel. You will go to school as usual, but when you come back you must make yourself very useful and do anything you are asked to do to pay for your board and lodging.'

Well, we moved in and were given a nice little bedroom in the basement. When I got back from school, I would put on a sack apron and clean the steps leading to the garden. The hotel was made up of four houses. In the front was one large door, but at the back there were four doors and four flights of steps to the garden. These were the ones I had to clean once a week. Then there was a lot of brass to clean, thick stair rods and brass nails along the corridor walls, and in the evenings I used to mend the bed linen. I never minded. I liked work and I liked sewing. I was really very happy and we ate well *every* day, and all the staff made a fuss of me. One waiter, who had been coming to the hotel each summer for several years, was very nice. His name was Louis. He once asked my mother if he should teach me to speak French, and my mother said, 'I would rather she perfected her English first.'

When we had been there about three months, my mother said, 'Your father keeps pestering me to go back to him, so I have decided to do so. I have told Mrs Cohen and she is quite willing that you should stay here, so you will be all right.'

'But mother,' I said, 'I can't stay here all be myself.'

'Don't be silly, child, you won't be by yourself; there will be dozens of people around.'

'Will someone share the bedroom with me?'

'I expect so. I have told Louis and he says he will keep an eye on you and see that you are not put upon.'

'I shall not like it here without you.'

'Well, I'm sorry my dear, but I must go back to your father.'

I did not even know she had been seeing him! However she left the next day. How could she? How could she?

One of the women workers shared the bedroom and *bed* with me and I went on just the same. Mrs Cohen was really very nice to me. I did not hear from, or see my mother again, until I suddenly felt I wanted to go home.

It was just before my thirteenth birthday. I told Mrs Cohen and she was quite angry and said that they had planned to give me a birthday party. Mr Cohen was going to do his conjuring tricks, and I could ask six girls from my school for tea. I said I was sorry but I wanted to go home. I can't think why I suddenly had the urge to go home, but I went, much to the consternation of my mother!

'Why have you come home?' she asked.

'Well, I wanted to be with you. I missed you.' I said.

'But you have been there nine months without me. Did something happen to upset you?'

'No,' I said, 'I just felt I would like to come home.'

'Well, it is very tiresome,' said my mother. 'I don't know where you can sleep. We have only the one room. I must go and speak to Mrs Brown.' Mrs Brown was the landlady, and what a darling lady she was to me.

Mrs Brown put a camp-bed up in her youngest daughter's room and said I could sleep there. Nellie was seventeen years old and she could have resented having me in her room, but she did not and was lovely to me. I was crying because I felt my mother did not want me. The next day was my birthday and she had no present for me, and I thought of all the nice things the Cohens had planned for me. I thought how stupid I had been to come away without first finding out if I would be welcome at home.

I don't think my mother ever wanted me! It was Hettie who wrote to the Home and told them our mother had remarried and that I should be sent home. Hettie was twenty-five years old and could take upon herself to go against my mother's wishes. I am quite sure it was against her wishes that I was sent home when I was eight years old. However, I soon slipped into the routine at home, and my mother made the best of a bad job, me!

Chapter 5

The next year passed quite uneventfully. I tried to help my mother in any way I could with the sewing, etc., but I had lots of spare time and would go on the beach and watch the Concert Parties. There were the Pierrots and the Highwayman and I could sing all their songs and repeat all their patter, but now my fourteenth birthday was approaching and my mother said, 'We must see about placing you somewhere.'

I had only left school six weeks when my mother told me I was to go to a position in London. I was to be a companion to a young married lady whose husband was away all day and she could not bear to be left alone! I am sure the companion title was just a courtesy title as I was more like a maid. I did all the work. My mother fixed me up with some nice clothes from Mrs Wragg and I had a sort of basket for a suitcase. The lid fitted right over and a strap was put round it.

My sister Annie came to fetch me. She was now twenty-three years old and I stood in awe of her. I enjoyed the train ride to London and then we took another train to Tulse Hill. Leigham Vale was only a few minutes walk from the station and '89' was the last house in the road, but the first one we came to. Mrs Bailey opened the door and the first thing she said was, 'My! She is small for her age.'

We all had tea together and Annie left telling me to be a good girl and do all I was told.

It was such a lovely house. One entered a large sized hall with two rooms on the right, the dining-room in the front with a large bay window, and the drawing-room next, with French doors to the very large garden. At the end of the hall a door led into the nice big kitchen and leading out of the kitchen was a scullery, a *walk-in* larder and a coal cellar. At the top of the flight of eleven stairs was a small sitting-room on a small landing, with a nice big window. Ada would sit in the room by her window and I would sit by my window, she crocheting and I sewing, and we would remark on all the people passing by, their clothes, etc. There were five more stairs onto a large landing, and over the dining-room was Ada and Ernest's bedroom and over the drawing-room was a billiard-room with a three-quarter size billiard-table on which Ada and I had many a practice game. Then there was a good sized bathroom and lavatory, and then my bedroom over the kitchen. There was another flight of stairs up to an attic, but that was not used until five years later when I had it. I was really happy in my little room and kept it so nice. Why I was put in the attic was because the Baileys took in a paying guest, a nice young man, Mr Knott. I think he was studying to become a teacher. After he left we had a Mr Band and he stayed for two or three years. It made a bit of extra work for me as he had breakfast and evening meal, but it is so lucky that I liked work, and still do, although I am now 94 years old.

I suppose my ten years at the Baileys was a very dull life for a young girl. The only time I was really free was on Sunday afternoons and evenings. I went to a bible class at Streatham and there I made friends with Jessie Tucker. She was about forty-five years older than me and looked very eccentric, but I loved her dearly and she loved me, and believe me I needed to be loved, as I myself had so much to give.

When it was my twenty-first birthday in 1913, I had a letter and an enamel brooch from my mother and a similar enamel brooch from my sister Annie. They were living together in Canada. I had a bit of crochet work from dear Hettie. I gave her one of the brooches as I did not want or need two. They were very nice brooches. Jessie got a very special tea for me and she had made her table look lovely. There were several little gifts, but the best of all was a beautiful poem she had written for me, and this is it:

A dear bright face upraised white flowers in hand
One brief moment thus, side by side we stand
And then a pleasant voice says soft and low
O Jessie dear I love, I love you so.
Right to my heart these words went gentle kind
And love wins love as mind responds to mind.
This happy thought will brighten many hours
This dear child friend has loved me, brought me flowers.

And when together in God's house I pray
Lord grant this love sincere abiding be
And lead us each Our Father nearer thee.
Oh friend in thy young life I see
Much promise rare choose ever God's pure way
Noblest and fair.
Stand firm to Principle and all that's best
Then thy life will be grand, sweet heaven thy rest.
Aye when time and time yearning for the love of one
Most dear yet far above me,
This dear child friend has brought me words of cheer
And God's flowers of comfort saying but I love you dear!

Jessie was the only real friend I had, but I had one or two friendly acquaintances whom I met at bible classes and one of them, Grace Boulton, asked me to take tea with her the following Sunday, which I did, and there I met Morris Towner who had celebrated his twenty-first birthday three weeks before mine. He was a very nice looking young man, about 5 ft. 8 in. tall, with blue eyes and lovely fair hair which curled all over his head. He took a great liking to me and asked me to meet him the next Sunday, which I did. This was the *first time* I had ever been out with a young man! I did not know what was expected of me. Ada Bailey told me to be careful, but did not tell me of what I was to be careful! I knew nothing whatever about sex. I don't think I had ever heard the word; in fact I know I had not.

Morris and I went out together each Sunday evening for nine months and I never even held his arm and never kissed, but he would send a box of chocolates during the week and a letter thanking me for the lovely wonderful evening! and we had done nothing except walk and talk. However, it petered out for the want of encouragement on my part and shyness on his.

I was very, very unhappy for a time and I did not go out with another man until four years later when I joined the Land Army. I think Ada Bailey was very pleased when Morris and I parted. She felt sure I would go on staying with her for we got on well and were very friendly together. If I ever spoke about leaving she would remind me of the terrible headaches I suffered and the painful periods, and would ask where else would I be able to rest when those afflictions were on me. So I stayed. The war was on and I was longing to do something for my country, especially as I had now met two of my brothers from Canada.

Frank the eldest, who was about twenty-eight years old, had joined the

Canadian Army, and Willie was twenty and he had come over against my mother's wish and joined the British Army. I only met Frank once until I had a message to say he was in a hospital in Northamptonshire and had had a leg amputated and would I go to see him. I did go to see him but alas I had one of my terrible headaches. I stopped at a chemist and asked the man if he could give me anything to ease it. He said he could not, so I went on to the hospital to see Frank and he, poor dear, was feeling rotten himself. I suppose I looked green and awful, for he asked me to leave. He said Hettie had been to seen him and she had had a leg amputated. He said her artificial leg squeaked and she went on about her operation, and then for me to come looking like death warmed up was more than he could bear!

The author at her mother's house in Montreal, 1920

Chapter 6

Well, at last I left the Baileys. I had been with them for ten years and five months, and in all that time I never heard a swear word or had a cross word from them. I was happy in a quiet way. Nothing very exciting happened except on one occasion, and it happened like this:

Now the Baileys were, we won't say mean people, they were careful, so when they went out for an evening I had to put all the lights out and just sit in the one room where there was a fire, and this was the billiard-room. This room was over the drawing-room, facing the garden, and with the thick curtains over the windows, the house looked to be in total darkness. About 8 o'clock I thought I would go down to the kitchen and get my supper. As I pulled on the gas-light, there was a man on the window-sill trying to undo the catch with a knife (it was a sash window). I froze for a moment and then I shouted, 'Mr Bailey, come quickly; there is a man trying to get into the kitchen.' The man jumped down and ran out of the garden. I put all the lights on and waited until the Baileys came home at 11 o'clock.

'What on earth is the matter?' they asked. When I told them, they praised me for my presence of mind to pretend I was not alone and they decided to get another dog. (Our lovely collie Prince had died a week earlier from a heart attack.) After that I was allowed to leave the hall light on whenever they were out.

The other thing that happened to disturb the dull routine was that when I was eighteen years old, just after my mother and sister had gone to Canada, I got rheumatic fever and I was ill for ten weeks. Ada got a friend, who was a partly trained nurse to come in the mornings to do things for me, and

Ernest looked after me in the evenings. Ada did not do a thing for me. She did not even come into the room, but would stand at the door and ask the friend or Ernest how I was. I myself seemed to be semi-conscious most of the time, but I was conscious of the awful smell of perspiration! I heard the doctor say my mother should be sent for and Ada explained that she had gone to Canada and was quite sure she would not come back to look after me, and of course she could not have afforded to do so, even had she wished to. Ada really was concerned about me and when I was better, she took notice of what the doctor said and would not allow me to do anything strenuous. I was not allowed to hold my arms up or shake mats, etc. on account of my heart.

The Baileys took me with them to Eastbourne for three weeks, and I remember I would just walk slowly down to the beach and only sit there doing nothing. It must have been better weather than we get nowadays, for I do not remember one wet day during the three weeks. I came back fully recovered, but the nice old Scots doctor told me I must always be careful, on account of my heart.

Chapter 7

Well, I was twenty-four years old when I joined the Land Army. Why I chose the Land Army I don't know, but I am glad I did because I loved it. A girl by the name of Janie Bridges joined at the same time as I did, and we were issued with our uniforms. This consisted of a pair of corduroy breeches, a khaki shirt and tie, two white overalls and a pair of boots. Later on we were given mackintoshes, but they were most unsuitable. They had cape sleeves and this we had to throw back when working, so of course our arms got soaking wet. In the Second World War the uniform was much more sensible.

Janie and I went to a place called Sutton Green, four miles from Guildford. There were already four girls there. We were lodged in a cottage and were looked after very badly by a young woman with a little boy of three years. We woke up at 5.30 and made a cup of tea and on our way to the farm we drove in the cows for milking. This was before the days of machine milking, and we two new girls were put onto a rubber udder filled with water to practise on. We got teased, but would retaliate by squirting them with water. However, within a few days I was given Daisy to milk and I enjoyed it.

When the milking was done we hurried the cows out before they dropped their 'pancakes', but we did not often succeed in doing this. We used to take it in turns. Three girls would wash up all the dairy things and the other three would muck out.

During the day we would do all sorts of things like ditch cleaning, cleaning out fowl-houses, for in those days, thank God, poultry ran free, so there were several fowl-houses, and eggs to collect. We returned to the cottage at 1 o'clock for dinner. Jane and I were there for six weeks and in all that time we never had any other pudding 'for afters' except stewed plums and custard. We all grumbled a bit and the woman would remind us that there was a war on.

At 4 o'clock we brought in the cows and the same routine was gone through again. By 6 o'clock we were finished for the day. We would go back to the cottage 'dying' for our tea, only to be told we could not have our tea as the baker had not been. Such bad management!

In the evenings I would do my bit of washing and I read a lot, but one or two of the girls would walk the four miles into Guildford to go to a dance or to the 'pictures' (cinema). The head girl, Janie, and I never did. We were glad to get to bed at 10 o'clock.

Except for the poor food and bad housekeeper, I was very happy during the six weeks we were there. Then we were taken to Chequers Court farm in Buckinghamshire, and there we joined ten other girls. We were all given new broom handles, and with these we stood in rows and walked along raising the corn which had been knocked down by the rain, ready for the reaper and binder to come along. This was before the days of combine-harvesters.

When the harvesting was over, Janie and I were asked if we would like to stay on as farm girls. We stayed, and to our disappointment we did all field work. From 6 o'clock in the morning until 6 o'clock at night we picked up potatoes, pulled swedes and mangel-wurzels from September to December. It was very cold, wet work. Our boots were not waterproof and although we rubbed dubbin on each night, our feet still got soaking wet. Even I was bored with the job.

When the other girls left after the harvest, Janie and I were the only two girls lodged in the lovely Ellesborough Manor, with Mrs Starkey as housekeeper. She told us that it was a training school for tractor drivers and that they had a number of girls there, but there was Halton Camp quite near and several of the girls had become pregnant so it was closed down for a time, but would open up again when they got a better class of girl. Well it was not long before girls began to arrive and they certainly were a 'better class'.

There were two daughters of a pre-war Colonel, a doctor's very pretty wife, and all the others seemed to have had first class education. Soon there were twenty-six of us at the manor and Janie and I were the only two doing 'farm' work. We had to start at 6 o'clock and finish at 6 o'clock for 18 shillings a week. 15 shillings of this was deducted for our board and lodging, which left us with only 3 shillings pocket money, whereas these girls being trained as tractor drivers had to start at 7 o'clock and finished at 5 o'clock. Also they got 6 shillings a week pocket money. So I told Janie I would see Miss Holden, the supervisor, and ask her if we could transfer to the tractor section. Janie said she too would like to transfer. Miss Holden seemed delighted to welcome us as tractor girls.

So when we came back after a short Christmas break, we started our training and I found it most enjoyable. We had a No.1 Fordson, the first Fordson brought to England and two American gentlemen came with it to teach us how to drive it. We had an overseer named Charmers. I never did find out what his job was – a sort of boss. We also had a master mechanic named Hain, and very good he was. The tractor was taken to pieces and he showed to us each part and explained what it was and its function. Then he put it all together again.

We had six weeks training. At the end of that time we could certainly drive a tractor, and most of us were qualified to do our own running repairs. I loved every minute of it, but felt rather guilty at being so happy when such a terrible war was still raging.

As tractor drivers we were paid 30 shillings a week and one shilling for every acre we ploughed and fourpence for every acre cultivated or for every acre of corn we cut. I just longed for the day when I would get onto a field and the farmer would say, 'There you are Miss; it's all yours.'

We girls certainly worked hard, but we also found time to play in the evenings. We got up a play or rather the Colonel's daughters did, and very good it was. We also used to congregate in each other's bedrooms for a good old natter and a bit of a midnight feast (rather frugal). We could have a log fire in our bedrooms, providing we chopped up our logs and cleaned up our fireplaces ourselves.

The manor was beautiful, and we divided it into sections by calling each part a different name. There was Percy's Parade, Sheepy Corner, Piccadilly Circus, etc. The colonel's daughters shared a room. Ranie the doctor's wife was the only one with a room to herself (I wonder why?) I shared a room with Hilda Garnett, Janie and a young actress we called Jumbo, who had a weak bladder and had to use the chamber-pot two or three times in the night. I was a light sleeper and would hear her and say, 'Poor Jumbo, not again!' and she would say she was sorry to disturb me. She said she was like a blooming horse, and would misquote a vulgar song:

Oh have you seen Jumbo make water
She makes such a lovely stream
She pees for a mile and a quarter
And you can't see our Jumbo for steam!

We made up rhymes about all the girls and they went like this:

We are the Government tractor girls
All sorts, all sizes, some straight, some curls,
Some tall, some short, some fat, some thin,
A jollier crowd has never been seen.

Our superintendent Miss Holden
Has hair of a beautiful golden.
She gave three the boot and told them to scoot
For staying out late with an old 'un.

Miss Smith of Percy Parade
On our alley has just made a raid.
We thought in our sport we would surely be caught
But in this a mistake we have made.

There was a young girl name Franze
Who thought she looked sweet as a pansy.
She trotted round Hain 'til she gave us a pain.
She wished she could stay out late like Mansee (our cat).

There is a young lady name Seaton
Whose face looks very worm eaten.
She is narky and cross and tries to be boss
But in all her high aims she is beaten.

Jumbo is the name we gave her when she came.
She is very big and fat and wears a very saucy hat.
Now she walks a trifle lame
For in her leg she has a pain.

There is a young lady named Lizzie
Who tonight is so very busy
Saying some prayers causing some stares
Because her hair is so frightfully frizzy.

There is a young lady named Ranny
Whose finger looks rather uncanny
For sad to relate it got squashed in a gate
And has grown very curvy and scranny.

There was a young lady called Worley.
She has very straight black hair
Which makes people stare
And that makes her wish it was curly.

There was a young lady named Hilda
Whom soldiers so greatly bewilder.
By way of a spree she ran up a tree
On a tractor which very nigh killed her.

Miss Goatcher is the lady's name.
On contractor work she gained some fame
By climbing hedges smashing gates
And by the tea-leaves telling fates.

Our tractor instructure called Hain
Is so decidedly vain.
He runs after girls with rat-tailly curls
Again and again and again.

There was a young girl called Watty.
Her appetite makes us feel grotty.
She munched and she chewed in a manner quite rude.
It's a wonder she did not drive us potty.

It was Janie from Sheepy Square
Whose fancy it was for short hair,
So to Aylesbury she went and her wages she spent
At a barber's establishment there.

Maureen is a girl we know.
At tractor work she is very slow.
She's got a job at 30 bob.
Let's hope such luck to us will flow.

There was an old josser called Chalmers
Who thought with his ways he could charm us
But we hate him like sin, because of his skin.
We have an idea it might harm us.

The six week's training passed very quickly and happily, and then we were sent to different places. Janie and I were sent to Abingdon and arrived there towards the end of February 1917. Lodgings had been booked for us with a Mr and Mrs Parker. We had to pay her £1 a week for board and lodging, and she also did our washing for this and would give us a cup of cocoa before bed!

A Mr Hayes met us and he told us he was our supervisor. He also said he was not quite ready for us so we could have the first week looking around Abingdon and 'enjoying' ourselves. We were the only two girls in Land Army uniform and we caused quite a sensation.

Abingdon in 1917 was a small rather dull little town with just one cinema. Janie and I were bored and very thankful when Mr Hayes called for us to start work. I was given instructions to go to a place called Bellesleigh and told to take my tractor and ask for a Mr Aldwinkle. There were several soldiers standing around in the depot and they watched Janie and me with amusement, so I was very thankful when the Fordson I was given started at the first swing of the starting handle.

I drove off very happily and when I had gone nearly seven miles, a farmer on horseback stopped me and said he was Aldwinkle and he would show me where the field was that I was to plough. We soon reached the field and he said those lovely words I had been dying to hear, 'There you are Miss; it's all yours. Get on with that!'

'How many acres?' I asked.

'Eighteen,' he replied, 'and I have marked it out for you, being your first time.'

This meant that he had stepped out the 22 yds. and put sticks up across the field to show me where to make my first furrow! I was so happy. I hardly knew how to contain myself.

Everything went well and I stopped at 1 o'clock for my sandwiches, then on again until 6 o'clock when Mr Aldwinkle came and asked me how I was going to get back to Abingdon. Do you know, I had not given it a thought! He said he would take me in the trap this time, but I would have to make some arrangement for my own transport.

When I went into the depot, Mr Hayes asked how I had got on and I told him. I said I would have to get a bicycle, and one of the soldiers said he would take me to a shop where I might be able to get a second-hand bike. Sure enough I did, a fixed wheel one for £1! I had never been on a bicycle in my life, so that evening this same soldier very kindly gave me a few lessons on bike riding. The others laughed at my bike and said it must have come out of the ark! I left it at the depot and walked the short distance to the Parker's house where we were lodging.

The place was nice and clean and the food was good. Janie and I were lucky to get into such good lodgings. Janie said she had been to a Mr Brain, just outside Abingdon, and that she had got on all right. We were both very tired and glad to get to bed at 9.30.

Mr Parker called us next morning at 5.15 as we had to start work at 6 o'clock. Janie walked to her field but I was helped onto my bicycle and set off on the seven mile ride to Bellesleigh. I wobbled a bit as it was my first ride, but I got to the field all right and spent another very happy day ploughing.

I finished the field in a week and Mr Aldwinkle was very pleased indeed. So was I. Not only had I tackled my first field without any trouble, but I also had 18 shillings extra in my wage packet, which meant that I had £2.8s.0d. I felt like a millionairess!

Chapter 9

Our unit consisted of a Mr Thomson, a retired country schoolmaster, who was the clerk; Mr Hayes our supervisor; and he had an assistant, a David Mitchell, who was a soldier recuperating from active service. There were 26 other soldiers, all recuperating. They seemed to spend a lot of time in the barn, at least there were always several there whenever I had occasion to go there.

The barn was a large building and several tractors were in it; a couple of Tysons, huge things needing one man to drive and one man on the plough. With the Fordson, it was a one man (or woman) job, as the driver worked the plough with a rope, by which one could lift the shears or drop them. There was also a caterpillar tractor there, a neat little thing which I had never seen before, but I was soon to get acquainted with it and drive it. A part of the barn was partitioned off to form a small office.

One day I was marking out a new field for ploughing and had just started on the first furrow, when Mr Hayes appeared with another man, a very smartly dressed man of about forty years old. I heard this man say, 'She will have a half moon by the time she is at the end of the furrow.'

I was furious and got off my tractor and I went up to him and said, 'I heard what you said. Why don't you wait and see the furrow before you pass remarks! Who are you anyway?'

He looked at me very seriously (I thought) and said, 'I am Mr Godwin, your boss, and you, I know, are Miss Goatcher.'

He offered me his hand, which I shook, murmuring an embarrassed, 'Oh!'

Mr Hayes was laughing as I went back to my tractor and ploughed a perfectly straight furrow!

It was not long after this that Mr Hayes disappeared and David Mitchell seemed to take over his job as well as keeping us supplied with paraffin and oil. Mr Godwin we saw on rare occasions. He was a District Executive Officer, and his chief job was to go round farms to make sure they were being properly run, and to see which meadows were suitable for ploughing up for corn growing.

As Janie and I had been together from the start and now were the only two land girls in Abingdon, it was natural we should keep together, but we did not have much in common. Janie did not seem to have any interests or hobbies, whereas I liked to read and sew and knit. It was not long before David asked us to go to the one and only cinema. After that we often went out, the three of us together, and I said to Janie, 'I don't really think David enjoys taking out both of us, so next time I shall make an excuse and not go with him. You are certainly more keen on him that I am.'

So Janie went with him and came home very miserable. She said that David had not been at all nice with her, and had acted as though he was bored stiff. So the next time David asked me, I went and he said what a job he had had to get me by myself. He said he had had to be almost rude to Janie to let her see that he did not want her. I was sorry, because at that time I was not at all keen on David and poor Janie was.

It unfortunately made things rather unpleasant when we were at the Parkers. Mrs Parker seemed to think I had 'stolen' David from Janie and was quite unpleasant to me, so I said I had better find other lodgings, which I did. Mr Thomson, who had always seemed to like me, said they had a spare bedroom and he would talk to Mrs Thomson and ask her if she would have me. He said he lived a couple of miles out of Abingdon at a village called Sunninghill, and his wife kept the post office. So I was quite glad now to leave the Parkers and move in with the Thomsons.

Mrs Thomson was a dear, and so kind. She was Mr Thomson's second wife. His first wife had died giving birth to her second son. The boys were now grown-up young men. The eldest, Billie, was a dear, kind hard-working chap, but slightly subnormal. The younger son was a good-headed business man working in London. I only saw him once when he came with his wife on a visit. I loved living with the Thomsons. Mrs Thomson treated me like a daughter. In fact she thought I would make a good wife for Billie and, because I chatted to him and now and again took a walk with him, I'm afraid he thought so too. But I had to get that idea right out of their heads.

David and I met most evenings, and it was towards the end of September that he asked me to marry him! I had grown to like him very much, but I was not madly in love with him. I was twenty-six years old and I don't think young men 'took to me'. They had nicknamed me 'The Duchess'. I had a feeling I was destined to be an 'old maid' and I did want to get married and have children. So I consented to marry David and he bought me a very pretty ring of turquoise and pearls, and I was very happy for a while. But in my heart I knew that David and I did not truly love each other. What love there was, was more on my side than his. He said he would take me home with him at Christmas to meet his family, but at the last minute he made excuses, and I felt I had had enough. So many times he had failed to keep appointments. So I wrote to him and told him we had both made a mistake and I sent back the pretty little ring and the one or two other trinkets he had given me.

I felt very miserable and it was very embarrassing when he came out to the field with paraffin and petrol, and he would beg me to change my mind and take back my ring. It was a relief to me when Mr Godwin said he had had David transferred to another unit. However, I was still very miserable and so would keep on working as long as the light lasted. There was nothing to hurry home for, as I was in lodgings and had not made friends with any of the other soldiers in the unit. In fact, they had all accepted that I was David's girl, so left me alone.

I began to notice that quite often when I was working late, Mr Godwin would overtake me in his car. He would stop and offer to tie my bicycle on the side of his car and drive me home. I was glad of the lift for I would have been on the field from 7 o'clock in the morning until around 8 o'clock at night, just stopping for an hour midday to eat my sandwiches. I used to make some tea by putting the tea leaves in a small can and drawing the water out of the radiator. It was quite drinkable! When I was ready to stop, I used to wash my hands by putting a little paraffin on them and wiping them on an old towel. It used to get all the dirt off and I was so used to paraffin that I did not mind or notice the smell. Then I would take off the very dirty overall and put on a cleaner one. The following week, this cleaner one came in for everyday use and the other one would be washed and become the clean one.

One night in May, I was cycling home and Mr Godwin overtook me and as usual stopped to give me a lift. He said, 'You work up to a very late hour, Miss Goatcher.'

'Well, I like work and I have nothing better to do.'

He said, 'You are very unhappy over David, aren't you?'

'Oh dear! I did not know that it showed.'

'Now don't be unhappy because David was not worthy of you,' he said. 'Some day a man will come along who will love you as you deserve to be loved,' and he told me later that he had no idea that he would be that man!

Chapter 10

I had finished ploughing in the Lasham district and I was sent to a farm fourteen miles away from Abingdon. If we had to work more than ten miles away, we had to get temporary lodgings. So I put the iron bands on my wheels, hitched on my plough, tied on my little suitcase and started off to this farm. I can't for the life of me remember the name of the place.

When I got there I found the farmer and he took me to the field to be ploughed. I told him I could not start until the next day as I had to find some lodgings. He said he thought I would have no difficulty, but I did have difficulty. I went to seven different cottages. At last a woman said she could put me up if I did not mind having Fry every night and if I would make my own bed. I said of course I would, and I would love Fry every night (wondering what Fry was!)

'You see,' she said, 'me and my daughter work on munitions and we don't get home 'til 6 o'clock.'

I was glad to get in anywhere, but this turned out to be quite comfortable and I really did enjoy fried sausages, or eggs and bacon, or liver and bacon.

I was there for three weeks, and Mr Godwin came out each week and brought my supplies, so I did not think it was funny for him to come. David had kept us supplied with fuel and I knew he had not been replaced. On my last day, he, Mr Godwin, arrived and helped me bolt on my bands for travelling. He took my suitcase and said he would leave it at my old lodgings, and that I was to go and work for a Mr Walker at Cumnor.

Mr Walker had a wife and six chidren, three boys and three girls, all a year or two younger than me. They were all very friendly and living at home, and I found that Mr Godwin was already on very friendly terms with them all. The first day I arrived, I was invited to take supper with them, and a very good supper it was. They seemed a jolly lot of young people, but alas Mr Walker was an alcoholic. He went to Oxford market once a week and what a job it was to get him home. Motor cars were not much in use in 1919, and Molly, the youngest girl, rode a motor cycle and side-car and she could take her dad into market. Once she asked me to go with her and help her to keep her dad from visiting too many pubs. Mr Walker sat in the side-car and I sat on the back of the bike holding onto Molly.

Mr Walker met us for lunch and then gave Molly £5 and told her to take me off. We were to go to the 'pictures' (cinema) or look at the shops and have tea, and be ready to pick him up at 5.30. Oh my, we tried to get him home before the pubs opened again. We could not and he went from one to another getting more and more drunk. Molly tried to plead with him: she told him I was very tired and had to be up at 6 o'clock next morning. He said, 'Tell Miss Goatcher to go to hell, and you can go with her.'

It got to nearly 9 o'clock and at last Molly said we would go home and leave him. So she went into The Randolf and told him we were going home. We had the surprise of our lives when he arrived home less than twenty minutes after we did. Both Molly and Mrs Walker were worried about me and I could not understand why they should be. However, Molly said, 'Come, Jess. I'll hide you in a barn'.

So I went with her and she made me get behind some bails of hay and said, 'Whatever happens don't show yourself.'

So I stayed quietly and Mollie went home.

Presently Mr Walker cantered by, waving his gun and shouting, 'Where is that bloody officious Miss Goatcher. I'll blow her bloody head off.'

Up and down he went for more than half-an-hour. Then his two eldest sons persuaded him to go home, telling him I had gone home long ago. A little later Molly came and said the boys had got him into bed and it was safe for me to go home. Mrs Walker was waiting for us with a nice supper and it was decided I would stay the night and sleep with Molly.

Next morning Mr Walker came into breakfast and he said, 'Miss Goatcher, my children tell me I was very rude to you last night. I am afraid I don't remember anything about it, but if I upset you I am very sorry indeed. I get these bad turns you know!'

I said, 'That's all right, Mr Walker. Think no more about it.'

I worked for him for more than six weeks and there were many 'bad turns', though not so bad as that one, and there were many very happy, jolly times. I had supper with them most nights, and Mr Godwin was often invited too, and he would take me home afterwards.

The next farmer I worked for was Mr Hayes. His farm was only two miles out of Abingdon. He was a quiet Christian gentleman. His wife had 'lupus', and her nose and parts of her face were nibbled away. I had a terrible shock when I first saw her. No one had prepared me for such a terrible sight, but she was a sweet gentle lady and I felt so sad for her.

It was now 1919 and the war was over. We 'Land Girls' were to be demobilised, so we went up to Reading and we were given a certificate and a few kind words and that was that.

The Manor House, Ellesborough

Chapter 11

I had of course seen a great deal of Mr Godwin since David left. I did not attach any great importance to the many times Mr Godwin came my way, but one Sunday in July I was working late to finish a field and Mr Godwin came onto the field and waited until I had reached the end of the furrow. I got off and I felt a bit mad with him turning up looking so immaculate, and I absolutely filthy. My white overalls I had worn all the week, and the first Fordson tractors had no mudguards and the iron spuds on the wheels used to send up lapfuls of earth, which mixing with the spots of oil on our overalls, made them look awful. It had been a very hot day and I was 'sweaty' and I must have smelt like a pole cat.

'Oh good evening, Mr Godwin,' I said, 'I'm afraid I must look as terrible as I feel.'

'To me you look a very cheerful but tired lady. Are you always so cheerful?'

'Oh no,' I said, 'I sometimes go off like a firework when I am upset.'

'What do you do with yourself on Sundays?' he asked.

'Oh I do my washing and wash my hair and all sorts of little jobs. Why do you ask?'

'Well, I was wondering if you would like to come for a drive with me. I usually drive round and look at the various farms in my area and my landlady puts me up a few sandwiches, so I have a little picnic on my own. I would like it very much if you would join me?'

I said, 'Thank you, Mr Godwin, but I could not do that. Whatever would the unit say if they knew you were taking out one of the tractor girls?'

He told me some months later that when he saw me looking so filthy and so cheerful, all of a sudden he realised that he loved me! He said to himself, 'My God, I love that girl.'

Well, he persisted in asking me to go with him on Sunday. At last I said I would and he said he would call for me at 2 o'clock. I said, 'No, don't call for me, I will meet you by Hayes Farm.'

I did not like to tell Mrs Thomson that I was going out with Mr Godwin because she was still hoping that her son Billie (who was a dear boy but slightly retarded) and I would eventually marry. I never entertained the idea for one minute.

Well, I always helped Mrs Thomson with the washing up after Sunday dinner, so it was a bit late when I set off to walk the three miles to Hayes Farm, and there was no Mr Godwin to be seen! I hung about for an hour and got a blister on my heel and a bunch of teenagers started singing a popular song of the moment, 'Kate, my beautiful Kate. I'll be waiting at the kitchen door!'

I took myself off in a huff and called on Mr and Mrs Watkins, who lived in Abingdon. I though it would give me a rest and a sit down before I started the long walk home.

They were so pleased to see me and said how lovely it was of me to spare time to visit two old fogeys like them. It made me feel mean and ashamed of myself. They gave me tea, which I needed. I made up my mind that I would find time to visit them sometimes, but not to make a convenience of them!

Mr Godwin came onto the field where I was ploughing next morning and I said, 'Where on earth did you get to yesterday? I hung about for an hour.'

'Well, where did you get to? I got to Hayes Farm at 2 o'clock and drove up and down for over an hour! However, we will not have any more of this nonsense. Next Sunday I will call for you at 2 o'clock.'

He did and we drove round the countryside and ended up at a place called Whittenham Clumps. It was up a hill and at the top were trees and nice grass to sit on. We had a picnic tea which his landlady, Mrs Roberts, had provided, and we sat and talked of this, that and the other, and before we knew it, it was 6 o'clock and time to start for home.

Alas, the car wouldn't start.

'If I sit in and steer, do you think you could give it a push Miss Goatcher? It's all down hill and should start.'

Of course I said yes and started to push. I pushed and I pushed for a quarter of a mile before the thing started. Mr Godwin was full of apologies.

'But my goodness, girl, you are a good 'un,' he said.

That was the beginning of many Sunday drives and it was during one of those pleasant afternoons that Mr Godwin told me he loved me. I was not too surprised because the times we spent together were so pleasant, but I was surprised when he said, 'Unfortunately I can't ask you to marry me as I am already married.'

'Oh no! Not you too.'

I believe David was married and that's why he made it so that I had to break with him. Mind you, I don't know for sure, but I think he was.

'Well,' said Mr Godwin, 'I am trying to get a divorce. I started doing so immediately after I realised I loved you that Saturday evening when you were finishing Hayes' field.'

'What! Have you been in love with me since then?'

'Well now,' he said, 'the divorce proceedings are hung up a bit because I can't find out her postal address for the papers to be served on her. I know she is living with a man called Beany and they have a smallholding and a few chickens somewhere outside Hastings!'

'Is there anything I can do to help?' I asked.

'Well you could, if you really would not mind trying?'

'Tell me what you want me to do.'

'Well,' he said, 'I will book you into a hotel in Hastings for the weekend and if you could wander out into the country, make discreet enquiries about Mr and Mrs Beany and get the right postal address. I will have to leave it to you to go about it however you are able to.'

Well, I went to this nice hotel and the weather was fine, but chilly, as it was now towards the end of September. I enjoyed a quiet Saturday evening but on Sunday I went out into the countryside and made various 'discreet' enquiries, but had no luck. I had asked the hotel to put me up a few sandwiches, so I found a quiet spot and sat and enjoyed these, and had a little rest as I had been walking for nearly three hours.

I started off again and it was not until nearly 4 o'clock that I saw a place that looked as if it could be 'the place'. I knocked on the door, which was opened by a tall plain woman whom I was sure was Mrs Allison Godwin! She had a little girl of three with her.

I said, 'Please forgive me for troubling you but is there a café or a village near? I have been walking for hours and I am dying for a cup of tea and a sit down.'

'Oh there is no village or café near here, but if it's a cup of tea you are wanting, I could give you that. So she made me a pot of tea and gave me a piece of cake. The little girl was very interested in me. She called me 'a pretty lady', the only time in my life I have been called that!

Presently her 'husband' came in and she said, 'This is my husband, Mr

Beany,' and explained to him about me hunting for a café.

'So,' he said, 'you took pity on her and asked her in for a cuppa. Just what you would do,' he said with a smile.

We chatted about this and that. Then I said, 'You are very isolated here. Does the postman come right out here with your letters?'

He said, 'Oh no. In any case we don't get many, but if there are any, they are sent to the post office in the village and we collect them.' (I felt like Judas.)

They did not seem to want me to hurry away, as they said they very seldom had a stranger to talk to, but I said I must go as it was a long walk back to the hotel. I offered to pay for the tea but they would not hear of it, but I managed to slip a shilling into the little girl's hand.

Albion met me at the station at Abingdon on the Monday afternoon and was most anxious to hear all about my weekend. He was very pleased to have a real address to send the papers to, but oh dear, I felt miserable, as the Beanys had been so nice to me and seemed so glad of a chat. I can imagine that Mrs Beany must have found it very loney, as there did not seem to be any neighbours, and where they lived was not a real cottage, more like a converted barn.

I found I could put off going to Canada for a year, and I wanted to stay on for a while as there was going to be an auction sale of our tractors and implements. It was well advertised and several of the farmers, for whom I had worked, said, 'Miss, if I buy your tractor will you come and work for me?' I asked Albion for whom I should choose to work and he said, 'None of them. I will buy your tractor in your name and you work free lance. Can you afford to buy a new plough?' Yes, I could, and I was thrilled at the thought of setting up my own contract ploughing business!

I worked each day painting the machinery ready for the dispersal sale.

'My' tractor went for £100 'to Miss Goatcher'. I bought an Oliver plough for £38.10s., and I was in business! I charged 27s.6d. per acre and I had more work than I could cope with. Albion kept me supplied with paraffin oil, petrol and oil. He would bring them out in the evening to whichever field I was working in and then I was finished for the day, and he would drive home to Sunninghill where I was still lodging. I was thoroughly happy!

Albion's divorce had gone through all right, but he had to wait 6 months for it to be made absolute, which was the law in 1920, so we thought it was a good time for me to go to Canada.

Chapter 12

It was ten years since my mother and Annie had emigrated and I had only had a few letters from them during those years. I had bought my ticket a year before and paid £20 for it, but I found the three other girls who shared the cabin with me had bought theirs six weeks before and had had to pay £26.

My sister Annie and my mother met me at Montreal and we had a taxi to St. André Street where they were living. My brother Willie was there, having been discharged from the Army at the end of the war. I felt I knew him better than Annie, as he and I had often met while he was in the Army and I was a Land Girl. He gave me a warm welcome and we all spent a pleasant evening with lots to talk about.

Next morning at breakfast, Annie said, 'You will have to get a job as quickly as you can, Jessie, because I cannot afford to keep you. I am already keeping mother, and Willie is out of work, so I am keeping him too.' It was not quite right that she was keeping mother, because I was executor of my Uncle James's Will, in which he had left £2,000 to each of his three sisters, and my mother told me she made her £2,000 straight over to Annie. £2,000 in 1920 was quite a large sum of money and in any case my mother did everything for Annie, and really worked jolly hard.

Now I had kept in touch with my old Sunday school teacher and she had written to a friend of hers in Canada and told her that I would most likely be in need of work. So that very morning, this lady called at my mother's house and said that her old mother, who was seventy-nine, wanted a companion, and would I like to go and see her mother.

'Why yes,' said my mother. 'I will take her myself, since she is quite a stranger in Montreal.'

So after a light lunch we set off. It was down West Mount, the better part of Montreal.

Mrs Magor took a fancy to my mother at once and asked her if she could take the job.

'I'm sorry,' said my mother, 'but I have my other daughter and the house to look after.' So Mrs Magor had to make do with me, but she seemed to like me and was certainly most kind to me.

It was a lovely apartment: a sitting-room, dining-room, kitchen, bathroom, and two bedrooms. A janitor cleaned the floors and windows and a Chinese man did the laundry. All I had to do was some simple cooking, a little dusting, and wait on Mrs Magor. I was free as soon as lunch was over, but had to always be back by 6 o'clock as she did not like being alone in the apartment in the evening. She would go to bed after a light supper and I would brush her long hair (of which she was very proud), and read the bible to her until she went to sleep.

It was very dull for a young woman, but I did not mind and Mrs Magor was most kind and generous to me. When I was going off in the afternoon, she would want to know if I was going to Ogelveys and if so, I was to have tea 'on her', which meant she gave me a dollar to pay for my tea. I was getting a very good wage, $65 a month, and everything included.

I was quite happy and was willing to stay as long as I was in Montreal, but Annie was not pleased. She said I ought to go home each afternoon, but it was a long bus ride and I was always worried in case I was late back, so I did not go home very often.

'You must leave there,' said Annie. 'You came here to be a companion to mother, not to Mrs Magor. I have found you a job with the Pycrofts, friends of ours. They only live on the next street so you can spend your time off at home. I have been putting in a drawer all the repairs and alterations I want you to do, so you will be able to get on with that while you are with mother'!

I ought to have stood up to her. I hated leaving Mrs Magor, but mother kept saying, 'Don't upset Annie'! So I most reluctantly left dear Mrs Magor and went to the Pycrofts.

They were gentlefolk and he was quiet and inoffensive. She was very mean and I was always hungry. She was very proud of the fact that she had been a Duff! which was an aristocratic family in England. I was only paid $45 a month and it was far more dull than with Mrs Magor, but Annie seemed pleased.

The Pycrofts had an island, consisting of 110 acres of uncultivated land. On it was a large barn and this had been converted into a really nice dwelling place. Mrs Pycroft spent six weeks there each summer and Mr Pycroft would come down for the weekends. The barn was not quite finished. There was a nice sitting-room and kitchen and their bedroom was complete but my bedroom needed quite a lot doing to it. Still, it was habitable. A French peasant family living across the river had owned the island and the Pycrofts had bought it from them. They must have also advanced money to the family, because the son, Demontini, was working on the barn whenever he could spare time from their own farm. They supplied us with milk, cream, butter and eggs and these were put under a shady tree, and we would row across at about 6 o'clock in the morning to get them. Fosh, the dog, would come with us and would always jump out of the boat for the last few yards, which he would joyously swim.

Before we got in the boat, Mrs Pycroft would set a net for the minnows and when we got back there would be 20 or 30 in it. I would have to pick the tops off the new grown bracken and we would have fried minnows and bracken tops for midday dinner, followed by a blancmange!

I was always hungry, especially as I was expected to dig the cabbage patch and pick wild strawberries, of which there were plenty. When Mr Pycroft came, Mrs Pycroft would play the piano and he would sing, turning the music for her. They were an old-fashioned loving couple. She once asked me if I had noticed how lovely his moustache was.

'He has never had it cut,' she said, 'and it is as soft as silk. If he were not my husband, I would allow you to stroke it, but you must take my word for it'!

I was glad when the time came for us to go back to Montreal, as I was eaten alive by mosquitoes and I was made to keep picking strawberries in the terrific heat. It seemed quite cool and pleasant back in Montreal.

I had now been in Canada for ten months and I was longing to get back to England, but I was having a job to save up enough money for my fare home. Then one day a letter came from Cooks, enclosing my ticket for home. Albion wrote and paid as he was tired of waiting, and would I come as soon as I could? I would have liked to have started at once, but Annie said, 'You can't go without paying Aunt Mary and Uncle Charles a visit.' So it was arranged that I should go to Cowansville to visit them.

It was the first time I had met them and they were lovely, old, in their 70s, and uncle had a long white beard. He looked like a beautiful prophet. They lived in a small cottage with a pretty garden which Aunt Mary loved. I stayed with them for six weeks, although I was longing to get home to

Albion. It was the happiest time in the whole of the eleven months I was in Canada. Annie had not been kind to me and mother would sometimes say (when we were alone), 'Try not to be hurt at Annie's ways. She has a very demanding job and came to it late, competing with eighteen-year-old girls straight from secretarial college. She is really very good!'

Chapter 13

I was now on my way home: eight days on the boat the *Scotia*, which docked at Southampton, and there was my darling waiting for me. We had to stay the night at Southampton and we put up at the Polygon Hotel. When I asked for a piece of bread with my dinner, the waiter said, 'If you have a piece of bread, madam, you won't be able to have any pudding.' I was shocked. I had forgotten how severely rationed we were in England. But it was now 1921 and the war had been over for two years. I can't remember how long the rationing lasted, but everything was in short supply.

Albion was still working for the Board of Agriculture. He had six more weeks with them. He was living at Wantage in Bridge House, kept by the two Miss Stevens and their brother. He had a bedroom and sitting-room, and the Misses Stevens cooked all his meals and looked after him well. He told me he had found a bedroom for me in a nearby house and I was to have all my meals with him, but I had only spent one night in the nice bedroom when the Misses Stevens said they had a spare bedroom if I would like to have it? Albion and I were both pleased about this, so I moved in.

I asked Albion what arrangements he had made about our wedding and he told me that he had done nothing.

'I thought,' he said, 'that you would like to be married in Brighton, at the church you attended in your school-days. So I'll take a week off and we will go to Brighton. You write to your mother's old friend and ask if she can put us up, but first my love, I must take you to meet my brother, Eustace, and my sister, Lou. At present they don't know about you.'

'Oh dear,' I said, 'I'm afraid it will be a big surprise for them and probably not a very nice one.'

So we went to Medstead. It was a lovely address:

'Cheerio, Blackberry Lane, Four Marks, Medstead.'

We arrived without warning, as telephones were not in many people's homes in 1921. They made us very welcome. They had a maid, so I did not feel so bad about them having to provide us with a meal.

Albion had told me once that his sister, Lou, was no good in the house. He said she left all the housekeeping to the maid. She looked and was a real 'old maid', about fifty years old, tall and plain looking.

'Fancy you calling my brother by his Christian name,' she said.

'Well of course I must call him by his Christian name as I am going to marry him!'

'Eustace,' she cried, 'Miss Goatcher says she is going to marry Albion!'

'Yes, that's right,' said Albion, 'I was going to tell you all about it when we had eaten.'

I laughed and said, 'I'm sorry, dear, but I had to explain to Lou how I had the temerity to call you by your Christian name.'

So Albion told them how we had known each other during the war, for about four years, and how I had gone to see my mother and other relations before getting married and now we were going to be married as soon as possible.

'Oh dear,' said Eustace, 'this does make things a bit difficult. You know I told you, Albion, that I had taken Down Farm at Preston Candover, and we move in on September 29th. What I shall have to do now is to get a job and a place for Lou and me and Jessie (the maid) to live in.'

'Why can't we all live together at the farm?' asked Albion. 'I've seen the house and it lends itself very nicely for two families, with rooms on each side of the hall and two kitchens.'

'Oh no,' said Eustace, 'that won't do at all. It would not be fair to your wife to have to start her married life with her in-laws.'

I was very glad to hear this as I would have hated to have to share with Lou, whom I could see had not 'taken' to me at all, but I did not say anything as I felt it was for Albion to settle it. Whatever he did, I would of course have agreed to.

'No,' said Eustace very firmly, 'You and Jessica will live at the farmhouse and I will get a job. It is now the beginning of August so I have no doubt I shall have found something by the end of September.' And he did.

He got a job as steward to a Mr Kennard, who was in the brewery business and he had become a millionaire through making a two per cent under proof beer for the soldiers, or something like that. I don't quite know what it was. Anyhow, he bought Preston House and 33,000 acres. There was also the lovely manor house where Eustace and Lou lived and a number of cottages for the work people, of which there were thirteen men.

Eustace was a very good steward and Mr Kennard thought a lot of him, and when, after several years, he sold the lot to Courages, he only did so after he had a written promise that Eustace could live rent free in one of the two modern cottages he had had built, and this Mr Courage very reluctantly agreed upon. It was a lovely cottage: three rooms downstairs, and three bedrooms and a bathroom! Even our ten roomed farmhouse did not sport a bathroom.

Lou had died some years before Mr Kennard sold the place, and Eustace lived in the cottage until he was eighty-four years old. He had a housekeeper, but she died before he did. His passing was very sad because he caused the cottage to catch fire and was burned to death. I grieved over his death. It was a dreadful end to a lovely man, of whom I was very fond.

'Have you realised, girl,' said Albion, 'that we may not be able to be married in church on account of me being divorced?'

'Yes, I have thought of it, but I am praying that we will find a vicar who will marry us. If we don't, I will not marry you as I will not be married in a registry office!'

'My dear, you can't mean that?'

'Indeed I do.'

'But what can we do, for I have a feeling that you will not find a vicar who will marry us.'

'Well, if we can't, could we not go through the marriage service together seriously and then I would live with you as though we had married in church?'

Albion was absolutely shocked. In 1921 it certainly was not 'done' for a couple to live together unless they were married. I am writing this in 1987 and I am shocked and saddened to know that it is now regarded as a normal thing, and to bring children into the world. Many women have three or four or more children, each with a different father. They seem to have no feeling of shame!

We got to Brighton and went to dear Mrs Brown, who hugged and kissed me. I said. 'Mrs Brown, we are not married yet.'

'Oh my lamb,' she said. 'Then I must find another room for the master's pyjamas.'

I said, 'We hope to be married while we are here and I want you to give me away.' She was delighted, but she did not ask how we were going to get married, and no banns had been called!

We went straight to St. Margaret's vicarage, but only saw the curate as the vicar was on holiday. He advised us to see the vicar of Brighton, the Reverend Pearce, which we did. He saw us in his study and somehow it was I who did all the talking and I found myself telling him that if we could not be married in church, we would live together after we had said the marriage service together, and he said, 'What is it you are keeping from me?' So then I told him all about what Albion had done and that he had never slept a night with his ex-wife or in fact had anything to do with her after the marriage ceremony.

'Is this true?' asked the vicar, and Albion assured him it was.

The vicar sat thinking for a while and then he said, 'I believe in you two and I think you will have a good life together, so I will marry you on Monday at 10 o'clock.'

'But,' I said, 'how are you going to make that right with your bishop?'

'You leave that to me,' he said. 'Now, we will get on our knees and pray.'

I almost ran back to Mrs Brown. She was nearly as excited as I was and said she would ask Edith Young (a girl with whom I had gone to school) to be the other witness.

The next morning, Sunday, the verger called, and my heart sank as I thought the vicar had 'slept on it' and had changed his mind! But what the verger said was, 'The vicar sends his compliments and could we make it Tuesday instead of Monday?'

I said, 'Yes indeed, but if it makes no difference, could we make it Wednesday and that would give me a little time to get a few things?' So it was arranged and we were married at St. Peter's Parish Church on 17 August 1921 at 10 o'clock.

'Oh,' the vicar had said to Albion, 'you will of course put bachelor!'

While we were getting married, Mr Brown, who had been a waiter, got a nice meal for us, and Nellie (Brown that was) was there and we had a nice little wedding breakfast. Then Albion and I went and sat on the beach and he said, 'I'm afraid I have a bit of a shock for you my love!'

I said, 'Is something wrong?'

'I had this letter this morning. You had better read it.'

Dear Mr Godwin,

This is to tell you we do not want Miss Goatcher or whoever she is, to come back in our house so will you please make arrangements for her to go somewhere else.

Yours truly,

the Misses Stevens.

'But why Albion,' I said, 'I thought they liked me, and they were so friendly and showed such interest in my trousseau. What can I have done or said to turn them against me?'

'It can be nothing you have said or done. We must just push it aside until we get back and then find out.'

Well, I felt it was no good worrying over it, so we spent a quiet uneventful few days. We both seemed quite content to sit on the beach and do nothing. I sent a cable to my mother to tell her we had married at Brighton and she quickly informed my dear Aunt Mary, who had said that if anything delayed the wedding, I was to go and stay with my Aunt Madge (my aunt's and mother's stepsister) whom I did not even know existed!

When we arrived back at Wantage and went into the sitting-room, I noticed the meal was laid for two! The Misses Stevens came in and Albion said to me, 'Sit down dear.'

'No, I am not going to sit down until the Miss Stevens have explained the extraordinary letter they sent!'

'Well,' said the younger one, 'we cannot understand how you can go off and be married in a week without having any banns called? It seems very funny to us.'

'Well,' said Albion, 'I assure you we are married and in a church to.'

'Look,' I said, 'I will show you my marriage certificate,' and I made to get it out of my bag.

'Don't you dare!' said Albion. 'If the Miss Stevens do not believe us we will leave their home at once.'

'Oh no, don't do that. Of course we believe you.'

So we stayed for the six weeks until Albion had finished his time with the Board of Agriculture and the Miss Stevens looked after us well, but I am sure they never believed we were married. I felt rather uncomfortable and would have been much happier if I could have shown them my marriage licence, yet it never entered my head to do so, since Albion had said I was not to.

Chapter 14

On September 29th Albion and I moved into Down Farm House – my first home, and very nice it was too: a fine, square built house. There was a porch at the front door, where one could put plants and a seat. The front door opened into a hall with rooms on either side. On the right was the dining-room and the kitchen, which had a red brick floor and a wood range, which I never conquered, and a bread oven. The large window looked out onto the duck pond and the stables beyond. On the left was the drawing-room and an office, and at the end of the hall there was a back kitchen taking up the whole width of the house. This also had a red brick floor and a hugh fireplace, which took up almost one side of the room. It would have burnt logs 4 feet long, but we never did have a fire there. There was a sink and a pump. We had a deal table 10 feet long, and on it we had the milk separates, etc.

Next to the office was a large walk-in larder with slate shelves. It was beautifully cold even in the summer. Upstairs there were five good rooms, four of them we furnished as bedrooms and the fifth, which was over the back kitchen and also took up the whole width of the house, we made into a billiard-room. Next to it was an indoor flush toilet, but there was no bathroom, which was not at all unusual in 1921 when we moved in.

We had very little furniture to start with and for a few months Albion and I shared the single bed, which was the only thing he had brought from his old home! The only thing we bought *new* was a double bed, otherwise Albion would go to farm sales and buy all second-hand stuff, even the pots and pans! I would have liked new cooking utensils, but I never grumbled. I was so happy at really having a home of my own.

The house was up a hill and there was a wind-break of lovely beech trees, planted in the shape of a horseshoe. I loved it and everything. I was so happy!

The land was poor and I have learned since, that it was ideal as a sheep farm, but we went in for everything, which was a great mistake. We grew oats, barley, and wheat. We had about 1,000 head of mixed poultry: chickens, ducks, turkeys and guinea-fowl. We had eleven cows, just ordinary shorthorns; four pigs, which I named Herbert, Arthur, Gertrude and Joyce; and four ferrets, which I named Matthew, Mark, Luke and Joanna! We had four horses and Jane the mule.

There was Carter and Jim the undercarter; Shepherd who was longing to have sheep to look after, but having none he filled in his time turning hedges and a hundred and one jobs, and he was a good conscientious worker. Then there was Stone, who was cowman and later I had Dolly, who helped on the farm and in the house.

It was all a failure from the start, but I was ignorant and did not know then that I was living in a fool's paradise! With hindsight I know we should have concentrated on sheep. Had we done so, we might never have had to leave, as we did alas, at the end of four years. But oh, how I loved those four years! I attended to the poultry, I made 50 lb. of butter each Tuesday (Albion taught me how to do it), and I would drive the tractor whenever I was needed. I was always busy and always happy!

We were busy cutting corn and worked late so as to finish the field (40 acres). As I got towards the middle, the rabbits started to run out. Poor things, they had been getting in towards the middle, as I cut round them. Albion shot some and the men killed them with sticks. They all thought it was great sport. Albion shared the rabbits out among the men. 'We are a bit late in finishing, but let's have you all here early in the morning so that we finish cutting the corn while the good weather lasts.'

Next morning we were all on the field by 7 o'clock except Carter. 'Where can Carter be?' said Albion. 'He is never late.'

Just then his stepdaughter came running across the field shouting, 'Oh come quickly, father's dying. Father's dying.'

Dolby and Albion and I jumped in the van and went across the field, the others following. Sure enough, there was Carter stretched out on the ground. The men picked him up and put him in the back of the van. I got in with him and had his legs in my lap. When we got to the farmhouse, Albion put the camp-bed in the cot, which was a tiny dwelling adjoining some more stables. I filled a stone hot-water bottle and put it at his feet, which were icy cold. The men were laughing at me and I could not think why they should, but I did not know then that Carter was already dead. Albion went down to the post office to 'phone for the doctor. We did not have a telephone in those days. The doctor lived at Alresford, seven miles away. He came at once and of course said that Carter was dead. It appears he had had some of the baby rabbit for breakfast and being a bit late, had hurried and then had a heart attack. His stepdaughter, poor girl, was dreadfully upset. He was the father of her two little girls and she was a bit simple, as was her dour old mother.

Of course they had to leave the cottage as we needed it for the new carter, and they all had to go to the workhouse. It made me very sad, but there was no way by which we could help it. The new Carter was named Vince and was not a nice man at all. If Albion took a day off to go hunting, they, Vince and the undercarter, would take advantage and would stand under the hedge at the end of a furrow and have a smoke and half an hour's rest.

One day I noticed from my view of the stables from the kitchen window, that they had been two hours over their midday dinner time. So I went out to them and asked why they were there for two hours. Vince was rude and said I was the Missus and not the boss, so mind my own business. I was furious and said, 'The boss will see you when he comes home.'

Of course I told all this to Albion and he told me to send Vince in to him when he came for the free skimmed milk which we gave them each day. I went in with Vince, and Albion said, whenever he was out or away, I was the boss, and they must obey me. Vince said he didn't take to being bossed by a woman, so Albion said, 'The remedy is in your own hands, Vince!' But Vince did not want to leave, so of course stayed, but I never felt safe when Albion was away, especially as I caught Vince stealing our cutlery! In those early days the only spoons and forks we had were real silver, from Albion's home and we only had six of each of those. Eustace had the other six as they had divided everything when Albion had married me. So I could ill afford to 'lose' any! The upshot was that Vince had to go and how thankful I was.

The four years we were at Down Farm were very happy ones for me. I did not know that we were losing money. Albion never discussed the financial position with me, but Eustace used to come over every Sunday and he and Albion would 'walk the fields' together, and I suppose they discussed the situation then.

I worked hard, but enjoyed doing so. On Tuesdays I made the butter and Albion and Dolly would wash and pack the eggs, not in containers which egg producers are provided with nowadays, but carefully in cardboard boxes. We would take in roughly a hundred dozen eggs, 50 lb. of butter, and any rabbits Albion had caught, and a few cock pullets. While Albion was at market, I would do my shopping and shop gazing and we would meet for lunch at the same restaurant each week. If Albion had finished his business, we would make for home, but if he wanted to meet farmer friends, etc., he would tell me to go to the cinema and meet him at 5 o'clock at the Horse and Jockey where he had put up the car or van, or horse and trap, whatever sort of transport we had at the time. When we arrived home, we would find the tea laid and in winter, the dining-room fire lit, for which we had to thank Dolly.

I have not told you how we came to have Dolly. Well Albion advertised for a man to help with the haymaking. I answered a knock at the back door and there was this small young woman.

'Is the boss in?' she asked.

'Well, no,' I said. 'What did you want to see him for?'

'It's about the haymaking job. What time will he be home?'

'About 6 o'clock,' I said.

'Right, I'll come then.' And off she went.

Now I knew she was married and I thought she was after the job for her husband. Anyhow, back she came at 6 o'clock. Albion was home and in the office, so I showed her in.

'Good evening, sir,' she said, 'I've come about the haymaking job.'

'For your husband?' asked Albion. 'Why did he not come himself?'

'It's not for he,' said Dolly. 'It's for me.'

'But I want a man,' said Albion.

'Have me, sir,' said Dolly. 'You'll find me as good as any man, better than some!'

'But you are so small,' said Albion, and turning to me he said, 'What do you think, girl? Shall we give her a try?'

I said, 'Yes, I think she is so keen, she ought to be given a chance.'

'Bless you, mam,' said Dolly; 'you won't regret it!' and we never did. She was strong and cheerful and willing.

After a few weeks she asked if she could live in the farmhouse.

'You see, mam,' she said, 'we have only a small cottage and there is my mum and me two brothers and me babe, and I have to sleep on the 'orsehair sofa.'

'Do you want to bring your babe with you?' I asked.

'Oh no. Me mum wouldn't part with her for the world.'

'Well, Dolly, I will speak to the boss about it and let you know.'

When I asked Albion he said, 'It's up to you, dear.'

So I told Dolly she could come. What a help she was to us. I taught her to drive the tractor and somehow she seemed to find time to do a bit of cleaning in the house. In fact it seemed as if she could not do enough for us to show her gratitude.

One of her brothers would call each evening and collect a pint of milk which we gave them for 'the babe'. Poor Dolly had the shingles and I made her stay in bed.

'Did Bill come up for the milk?' asked Dolly.

'I think it was Bert who came, and he has a bad eye.'

'Oh no,' said Dolly, 'that wouldn't be Bert, that would be Bill.'

'Well, Dolly, I have a job to tell one brother from the other, but I still think it was Bert.'

Next evening Dolly was up and Bert came for the milk,

'Hello Bert,' said Dolly. 'How's Bill's eye?'

''Tain't Bill's eye; it's my eye,' said Bert.

'Oh no. Well what's the matter with it?' asked Dolly.

'Well,' said Bert, 'I was putting some Stockarn Tar in the 'orse's hoof and some got in me eye and it don't half hurt.'

'I bet it does,' said Dolly, but without much sympathy in her voice. She did not like her brother Bert, but she loved her Bill.

The author, at work for the Land Army, at Chequer's Court, Buckinghamshire, 1917

Chapter 15

We left the farm on 29 September 1925. We were there for only four years. I was heartbroken. I asked Albion why and he said we were losing money all the time.

'What are we going to do and where will we go?' I asked.

'Well,' said Albion, 'I'll see Mr Hope and see if he will rent us that 88 acres and the cottage up at Wield.'

Mr Hope lived with his mother, Lady Hope, in the 'big house'. He owned a lovely wood of 250 acres and this bit of farmland of 88 acres. We had become very friendly with him, and he and Albion had spent many evenings playing billiards, and if it got too late when they had finished playing, he would stay the night. I always kept a bed ready. Lady Hope was very reduced in circumstances and the only staff she now had was her old lady's maid who now did all the work and cooking with just the help of a charlady two or three times a week. Mr Hope said they locked the house up at 11 o'clock and he could not disturb them. So that was why he slept at our place sometimes.

It was the day of the farm sale and I got up with one of my migraine headaches! Thank goodness Olive Rabbetts helped me to keep the drinks going for customers and friends. Albion seemed really annoyed that I should have a headache on that day. He could not have hated it more than I did! We not only had the farm implements, cattle, horses and poultry to sell, but most of our furniture, because we were now moving from a ten roomed farmhouse to a four roomed cottage. I was very sad to see our things go.

We went up the hill about two miles to Wield and it was not long before we were settled in, but life was difficult as we had had to sell so many of our farm implements. It made farming without the proper tools very hard. I did my best, but I did feel a bit peeved when Albion spent a lot of time and some money on building himself a garage. It seemed unthinkable in those days to leave the car just outside the 1925 cottage, but nowadays in 1988 one can rent *space* for a car!

Albion had a farmer friend living in Kent and it was arranged that Frank would send 4,000 sheep up to us and Albion would allocate them out two or three hundred a farmer, depending on what feeding pasture they had. The farmer got six shillings and sixpence a score and Albion got sixpence for every returned sheep. If the farmer looked after the sheep, there would only be a loss of say one per cent. Albion would ride round the farms and look at the sheep, and if they looked all right he would not bother to see the farmer, but sometimes we found one or two had had the blowfly on them. Then I would have to get the sheep between my knees and clear off all the maggots which were eating into the rump and then put Stockarn Tar on the place. Poor things, the tar must have stung, but it was awful to see the hole that the maggots had made. I used to feel and be sick doing them, and why I did them and not Albion I don't know. He would catch the sheep for me! Sometimes I had to dose them. We would have a pail full of medicine; what it was I don't know, but I would fill a small bottle and open the sheep's mouth and pour it down her throat. Anyhow, whatever we did must have been the right thing, because Frank sent them again the next year and Albion seemed pleased with the sizeable cheque he got.

Well, we struggled on for two and a half years at Wield and then had to give up. We were fighting a losing battle.

'What are we going to do?' I asked 'Could you not get a job as farm manager, as Eustace has?'

'No, girl,' said Albion, 'I could never work for a boss.'

'Well what about when you were working for the Board of Agriculture?'

'That,' said Albion, 'was quite different from working for a master.'

'Well, what we are going to do? We have to leave here in two weeks time?'

Before the First World War, a wealthy German named Schutz bought the whole of Wield Wood, about 310 acres, and he had two beautiful cottages built, one in Wield and the other a mile or two away. His intention was to have a driveway built from one cottage to the other and have a large house built up in the woods. He got the cottages built and part of the drive, and then the war came and he had to sell it. Mr Hope bought the Wield cottage and 250 acres of wood, and a London solicitor bought the other cottage and 60 acres of wood.

Albion got in touch with the London solicitor and asked him if we could rent the cottage and wood. He came down to see us and he said he would like to sell it and had it advertised in the local and London papers. We could rent it at 12s.6d. per week and we could shoot pheasants, rabbits and pigeons, and if any prospective buyers came would we show them round. Of course we would!

It was a cottage exactly like the one at Wield, but this was right on the edge of the wood. Ten yards to the little wicket gate and we were in the wood! It was paradise! – and the happiest ten months I have ever spent in my life. We had a few chickens, and the pheasants became so tame. They would come and feed with the chickens. I used to wander in the wood and could not avoid treading on the primroses and bluebells. Our two dogs, Donald and Nellie, were well trained and they would sit quietly with me or go sniffing around, and one word would stop them chasing the rabbits and hares.

This cottage had no water and the only water we had was rain water caught in butts. For drinking we had a filter. We had to be very careful with water: no rain, no water! I would have been happy to live there for ever, but of course it was impossible. We had no money coming in, only a pound or two we got at market for rabbits and hares and a few eggs.

We kept talking about what we were going to do. Albion seemed to like the idea of a café and we did go and look at one or two which were advertised.

One day while we were having our dinner, which we always had at midday, a beautiful car drew up at the gate and a large man and small woman got out. The car was driven by a uniformed chauffeur. Albion went to the door and the man said they had come to look around the property.

'But I see you're at your dinner so the Misses and me can sit in the car 'til you've finished.'

So I said, 'Would you like to join us? We have plenty.' This they were pleased to do.

'What about your chauffeur?' I asked.

'Oh, he'll have sandwiches with him. Don't worry about 'im!'

After dinner Albion took them through the wood, and an hour later they left saying they would talk it over and come back next week about the same time. I took the hint and cooked enough dinner for four! but I said to Albion, 'These people won't buy.'

Well, they came and enjoyed the roast lamb and home-grown vegetables. The man, his name was Arnold, said that *if* they bought, he would have a large house built in the wood.

'But wat are you going to do when you leave this 'ere place?'

'Well,' said Albion, 'we thought we might buy a café. My wife is a good cook and very clever making cakes and pasties.'

'You're right,' said Arnold, 'and you don't want to waste yer time cooking for no café. We've got just the place for you in Bath. It's an apartment house and the Misses' sister 'as 'ad it for 41 years and it ain't on the market yet. It's yours! With your Misses being able to cook like she does, you're made!'

'But what is an apartment house?' I asked.

'Well, the ladies or gents have two bedrooms and a sitting-room.' Course it's usually a couple of sisters or a mother and daughter, and they buy their own food and you cook it for them. You 'as two maids: one to help you in the kitchen, and the other to make the beds and take up the meals. Now you two think about it and we will come back next week and go into all the details.'

'What about the property here? Are you interested in it?' asked Albion.

'Well, no,' said Arnold. 'It's a bit too isolated really and 'aving no water is a great drawback. But we'll be along in a day or two and I'll 'ave all the details for you, Mr Godwin, about the Bath house, and you and your Misses talk it over. You'd be mad to miss a chance like this. Mrs Garraway wat owns the place now (she's my Misses' sister), she ain't never had to advertise. She can keep the 'ouse full. Only lately, at seventy-three years old, she's eased off a bit, but you with the 'ouse full, you'll make money.'

Well, Albion and I talked it over but we did not really know anything about it and thought we would have to see the place before we decided. Anyhow, Arnold and his wife came again in a few days time and he had drawn up a contract which he wanted Albion to sign. I said, 'I must look at it too, especially as it seems as if I am the one who is going to do the work!' The contract said we were to pay £1,000 down and £1,000 for the Good Will and I think it was £60 a month for fifteen years. Then, Arnold said, we would have paid for the house and, said Arnold, 'I have totted up your expenses and at the end of the week you'll have 4s.6d. over.'

'But,' I said, 'you have not allowed anything for food for us and there will be four of us to feed.'

'Oh you don't have to buy no food for yourselves.'

'Really!' I said sarcastically. 'What do we live on, love and fresh air?'

'No need to be cheeky,' said Arnold. 'What you does, is take a little from each of the people upstairs. If you 'as to make the rest of the joint into rissoles, you keeps back four or five and when you takes a pint of milk for each of them, you take a little out and they never know about it. You'll soon get into the knack of it. Mrs Garraway, she never had to buy no food for herself or the maids.'

I said, 'I will never get into the knack of it because I will never do it. I have never stolen anything in my life. I am not going to start now.'

'Don't be silly,' said Arnold. 'This ain't stealing. This is taking your perks.'

'I don't care what you call it Mr Arnold. It is stealing and I am not going to do it.'

'Well,' said Arnold, 'you are going to get into debt and have a lot of worry.'

'Then I must just do the best I can,' I said, 'but I will not take anything that does not belong to me.'

The next time he came, Albion said he ought to see his solicitor and show him the contract that Arnold had drawn up.

'No,' said Arnold, 'you don't want no solicitor, you're dealing with friends.'

Albion let it go at that and signed the contract, but I said he was not really a friend as we didn't know anything about him except that he was certainly not an honest man, or a man with principles.

Chapter 16

Well, we arranged to move into the house, Hillside House, 35 Belvedere, Bath, on the 28 July 1928, but it was arranged that I should spend two days with the Arnolds at their flat in Bath and Mrs Arnold would take me each day to the house to see how Mrs Garraway ran it.

Mrs Garraway took me upstairs and showed me one or two of the rooms and said she could not show me the others as the ladies were in them. 'Well won't you take me into them and introduce me to them?'

'Oh no,' she said, 'I can't do that.' I did wonder why she could not, but I did not press her.

The kitchen, although in the basement, was nice and bright, and there was a kitchen range with a bright fire burning and the most beautiful dresser filled with beautiful blue china. It was not until I took it down to wash it that I found every plate was broken and chipped. On the top shelf there were eight decanters, on the next, tumblers and wine glasses, etc., and on the lower shelf, small fancy dishes, etc., and underneath there were three lovely brass jugs and two brass cans and *very* large white enamel jugs, which I was told had to be taken up filled with hot water, to whoever wanted a bath; for in the very beautiful house there was no bathroom.

Well, running along side of the kitchen was a stone passage, separating the scullery, and along this passage I saw a cat's messes and wet cloths on the ground, which I remarked upon.

'Oh,' said Mrs Garraway, 'that's that upstairs maid, Lily. She's a filthy little slut and she's under notice to leave. She has only got two more weeks, then you must go down to Mrs Maidment, at the Registry Office, and get another girl. She always has plenty on her books.'

I also remarked that her cat was not house-trained! She said, 'I'm having him put to sleep. You'll be bringing your own I suppose?'

'Yes,' I said, 'I will, but are you troubled with mice?'

'Well, there's bound to be the odd one or two,' she said.

'I don't worry about mice, but if you had black beetles, nothing would induce me to take the house. I hate beetles more than anything!' and Mrs Garraway never said a word!

It was now nearly 12.30 and Mrs Garraway said, 'Annie, you must take Mrs Godwin away now as I have to be busy with the dinners.'

'But surely, 'I said, 'this is just the time when I should stay and see how you go on?' But she would not let me stay and the same thing happened next day, so I told the Arnolds there was no point in my staying any longer. So I went home and how lovely it was to get home to the lovely little cottage. Albion was most anxious to know how I had got on and he did not seem to mind that I had not been introduced to any of the ladies, or to watch while Mrs Garraway cooked the dinners, but somehow I minded very much, especially at not meeting the ladies!

Well, we started packing things up and Albion went into Basingstoke market with our hens – all except Princess, who was sitting ten eggs.

'What will we do when the chicks are hatched?' I asked.

'Well, we shall have to take them with us,' said Albion.

As each day passed and the time drew near for us to leave, I got more and more depressed. We had arranged to arrive on the 31 July 1928 and said we expected to get there at around 8 o'clock in the evening.

We loaded up the Fiat Tourer and had Donald the retriever, Nellie the Jack Russell, Pretty Sarah the cat with her kitten Pollyanna, and Princess and her ten chicks. How and where we got them all in I don't know. It took us longer than we had thought it would to clear everything up and load up the car, and it was around 8 o'clock when we left and past 11 o'clock when we reached Bath! We had of course to stop once or twice to let the dogs out.

The Arnolds, who were waiting at the house for us, were nearly frantic with worry. What they would have done if we had not turned up, I don't know, as Mrs Garraway had already left! They told us to be very quiet as everyone had been in bed for hours. They said there was a bed made up at the top of the house and they left.

We had by now brought in the animals and essential things. Princess and her chicks were all right in a box, also Pollyanna. There was a door at the bottom of the stairs, so there was no fear of the pets getting upstairs, so we turned them loose in the basement, and how curious they were. They sniffed about everywhere and there were lots of nooks and crannies for them to explore. We prepared a meal for each of them, and then we cooked eggs and bacon and made a pot of tea for ourselves. The kitchen range was still burning and the kettle singing on the hob. We had had nothing to eat since our simple tea at 4 o'clock, so we enjoyed the meal very much.

I said to Albion, 'We can't possibly go upstairs to sleep and leave the pets down here by themselves.' So we went to look at Mrs Garraway's bedroom, which led off the sitting-room. It was a nice little room overlooking the garden, but the state of it! The soiled sheets were still on the unmade bed and the washing water still in the basin on the washstand!

'Well, that room is out of the question for tonight,' said Albion. 'What can we do, girl?'

'Well,' I said, 'it is now gone 1 o'clock and we have to be up before 7 o'clock as the maids are due down at 7 o'clock, so I think we had better just doze on the armchairs in the sitting-room.' That is what we did, with all the pets around us, and we woke around 6 o'clock, which was our usual time for rising.

There was no sink in the kitchen where we could wash, so we had a bowl on the kitchen table and managed like that. Our furniture was due to come that day and sure enough it arrived just after 1 o'clock, and I left Albion to attend to that. But I must tell you about the first morning!

The girls came down and we told them who we were. Peggy the kitchen maid was nearly fifteen years old and looked a nice bright clean girl. Lily the upstairs maid was unwashed and mucky looking and I was glad that she was under notice to go, for I could see she would not suit me.

I said to Peggy, 'Peggy, I am quite new to this work, so I shall have to rely on you to help me. Will you do so?'

'Oh yes, mum, I'll help you all I can. The ladies don't have their breakfast until 9 o'clock, but we has ours as soon as Lily has taken round the hot water for them to wash with. I has to get the range going first thing as that is the thing the cooking is done on and supplies all the hot water. For breakfast we has two rashers and an egg and we can make ourselves toast. The ladies mostly have toast and tea and just a boiled egg. At 10 o'clock each morning you 'as to go up to the ladies and see what they wants for dinner. They goes out and buys it themselves, but you have to cook it.'

'Thank you Peggy,' I said, 'that will be enough to be going on with. I am going to clean the little bedroom ready for us to sleep in tonight. Mr Godwin will cook the breakfasts, and Peggy, I would like you to say 'sir' to Mr Godwin and address me as 'madam'. I object to being called mum. Is that all right with you?' I asked with a smile.

'Oh yes, madam.' she said.

Meanwhile Albion had been cleaning out the furniture from the bedroom and sitting-room. There were lots of places in which it could be put for the time being until we could decide what to do with it. One of the clauses in the contract was, that we were not to get rid of anything until we had finished paying for the house. So we packed Mrs Garraway's old stuff, which of course was now ours really, as we were supposed to have bought the house and *contents*. Meanwhile the two dogs and the cat, Pretty Sarah, had been inspecting the garden which I saw led into a park. But with the garden gate shut, the pets were quite safe. Albion had put Princess and her chicks in the garden too, and they were able to peck around.

I cleaned the quite pleasant (small) bedroom overlooking the garden and made up our own bed with the nice clean sheets. I thought, 'How nice it will be to get into that tonight!' Albion and I had rather a hurried breakfast in the sitting-room, which also overlooked the garden. Time was getting on and I did not want to be late on my first visit up to the 'ladies'!

I went first to Mrs Halford, who lived on the hall floor with her stepdaughter, Kate, who was seventy-three years old. Mrs Halford was eighty-three. She was a small, plump woman dressed in a good black dress with a lace collar and a square of lace on her head, which was quite bald on top, but the lace cap looked very nice and her white hair each side was curled with the (now) old-fashioned curling tongs. The old lady gave me a polite but by no means friendly greeting. I learnt later that Mrs Garraway had always said, 'Yes mum, no mum,' and gave her a little 'bob'.

I then went up to the two Miss Grieves. How different they were! They both shook hands and hoped we had settled in all right! They were two wizened little ladies and I grew to love them.

The Halfords said they would have steak with parsley butter potatoes and beans, and an egg custard to follow. The Misses Grieves said they would have halibut with sauce, potatoes and carrots and a sponge pudding. I then went up to Miss Gordon, who was only in for a month. She played the violin at the Bath theatre. She greeted me very warmly and when I asked her what she wanted for dinner, she asked if I could give her some of whatever we were having. This was easy.

I came down and told Albion all about the ladies and then sent him off to buy a joint for our dinner. I felt I could manage the cooking that day as it was fairly straight forward, but it would have been nice if the pots and pans had been in better condition. I had to do most of the cooking on the range. There was a gas stove, but it was a very old one and like everything else, very dirty.

I got the dinner up by 1 o'clock and then we put the maids' dinners ready, and got our own.

Peggy said, 'Mrs Garraway had her food in the kitchen with us.'

I said we would have ours in our own room, which we did. Peggy said, 'They upstairs has their tea between 4 and 5 o'clock: just thin bread and butter or buttered toast, but we girls does that. You don't have to bother 'cos you 'as to start on the evening meals about 6 o'clock.'

I had found cooking the different things and having to get them all up at 1 o'clock quite a strain, and I wondered however I would cope when the house was full, which it would soon have to be to enable us to make ends meet.

As Peggy was sweeping the kitchen floor, I saw crumbs along the edge of a box where the coal was. I said, 'Peggy, I know you cannot raise the box to sweep the crumbs away, so I will raise the box for you to sweep.'

I raised the box and was shocked to the core, for underneath was a living, seething mass of black beetles! Peggy and I stamped on them, but they scuttled away. Peggy looked shocked and I felt physically sick after stamping on the beetles.

'I ain't moved that box since I been here,' said Peggy.

'Well, we will do away with it altogether,' I said. 'It seems to me a daft idea to fill a coal hod and then tip it into the box, which you then have to shovel onto the fire.'

There was a recess on the left side of the range, with shelves.

'What about these shelves?' I asked Peggy.

'Oh I ain't never touched them.'

In 1928, when one bought rice and sugar, etc., it was weighed and put into a sturdy blue bag. Everyone of those bags contained not only sugar, rice, etc., but black beetles! How Mrs Garraway had managed, I don't know. Did she just knock the beetles out and use the contents? I threw the whole lot away and sent Albion out to buy tins or jars or whatever he could. After this it was a constant battle against the beetles. We would put Keating's powder down at night and sweep up a dustpan full each morning, and they never seemed to get less. We have pest controllers now but if we had them then, we knew nothing about them.

The beetles were everywhere. Each night as I went into our bedroom, I would pray, 'Please, Lord, don't let there be anymore beetles,' but there often were some and I went on fighting them for seven years. Then one day, when I went into the chemist's just up the road to buy more Keatings, Mr Moore the chemist asked, 'What do you do with all the Keatings you buy?'

So I told him, and he said, 'I can sell you something far more effective than Keatings.'

He sold me some Blatus. It was a phosphorous paste, and one had to put some on bits of cardboard and push it into any cracks one could find, and one could find plenty of them. There were cracks where the stove joined the wall and where the wooden floor ended and the stone hearth started. There were cracks in plenty. I went to work on them each night before I went to bed and in two weeks there was no sign of a beetle, dead or alive! It was just wonderful! I lived in that house for forty-three years and I never saw a beetle!

Chapter 17

Two weeks after we arrived, I went up to Mrs Halford for 'orders'. She said, 'When is Mrs Garraway coming back?'

'Mrs Garraway won't be coming back. We have bought the house,' I said.

'You deceitful little upstart,' said Mrs Halford. 'This is your doing. Mrs Garraway would never do a thing like this: leave us without telling us she had sold the house!'

I said, 'Mrs Halford, how dare you say these things without knowing the circumstances. We had no idea that you had not been told that the house had been sold to us. We did all the business with Mrs Garraway's brother-in-law, Mr Arnold, but when I came for a couple of days to see how to 'run' the house, I asked Mrs Garraway to introduce me to the ladies and she said, "Oh no, that would not do; I can't disturb them!" '

The Halfords were with us for six years and the old lady was most unkind and sarcastic towards me all the time. Albion called her the 'Saintly Devil'. She would toddle off to early morning service once a week and if she could not go, she would have the vicar call to give her Communion, and she would sit by the window reading her bible. She looked sweet, with her pretty lace square over her bald patch, and people would remark on the sweet devout lady in the front room!

Miss Halford, the stepdaughter, was a saint and she tried to smooth troubles between Mrs Halford and me. There was the time when some new people moved in and Miss Halford read the name on the luggage, 'La Trope Bateman'.

'Dear me,' she said, 'one of my stepmother's relations was a La Trope

Bateman. I wonder if they are a relation.'

It turned out Mr La Trope Bateman was a relation, so on his birthday, New Year's Day, Mrs Halford invited them to midday dinner. She ordered artichoke soup, roast chicken, sausages, bacon, bread sauce and gravy, roast potatoes and spinach, an apple tart and cream. I was relieved that there was nothing that I could not manage, though I knew the artichoke soup would be a nuisance. (In the 1930's I don't think there were tins of soup. If there were, I knew nothing about them. I always made all the soups.) Of course, in addition to this meal, I still had the Misses Grieves' meal and Miss Talbot's! Still, I had by now got fairly good at cooking the different meals.

Next morning I went first to Mrs La Trope and she said, 'My dear, that was a lovely meal you sent up yesterday. Mr La Trope and I enjoyed it so much. I am going out to buy you a little present to show how much we appreciated all your efforts.'

I said, 'Just to know you enjoyed it and are kind enough to tell me so, is present enough for me.'

You can imagine my shock when I went in to see Mrs Halford and she greeted me with, 'Well are you not ashamed of yourself?'

'No,' I said. 'Why should I be?'

'Well,' she said, 'that dinner yesterday was ludicrous!'

'How funny,' I said. 'Mrs Bateman has just complimented me on it and is going out to buy me a little present.'

'Well, I have already sent Mrs Beazer (the woman who came in each day to help her to dress) out to get you a present.'

'How strange,' I said, 'to give me a present if you are so disgusted with my cooking.'

'Show her what you bought, Mrs Beazer,' and Mrs Beazer gave me a large parcel.

'Open it, open it,' said Mrs Halford, and I opened it to display a hair sieve.

'Now,' she said, 'next time I order spinach, perhaps you will be good enough to put it through the hair sieve and serve it with cream, not chop it and put a dob of butter on it!'

'Mrs Halford,' I said, 'I have six hair sieves downstairs, all different sizes. What I want is the *time* to use them. You seem to forget that I had three other different dinners to cook besides yours, all wanted at one o'clock. You keep your sieve and next time, come and put your own spinach through it. I think you are a very horrid woman.' And I hurried out of the room before I burst into tears.

Albion found me and asked what was the matter and when I told him, he said, 'Good for you, girl. I'm glad you spoke up to the old hypocrite.'

'Yes,' I said, 'but supposing they leave.'

'Don't worry about that, my dear, they won't leave until one of them is carried out in her box and if it's the old hypocrite, she will die on Christmas Day, just to make things awkward for us.' And would you believe it she died at 4.20 on Christmas morning 1934! I sometimes wonder if Albion was psychic!

Dear Miss Halford came and tapped on the beige door that led to the kitchen, so I went to answer it and I said I was so sorry. She said, 'Oh please go and apologise to madam!'

'Good gracious no,' I said, 'I expect Mrs Halford to apologise to me! I meant I was sorry for the unhappiness I've caused you.'

'Yes,' she said, 'the atmosphere is awful.'

Mrs Halford never did actually apologise, but a week later she offered to 'treat us' to an afternoon coach trip! She often called me an 'upstart' or 'one and one usurper'. She was Miss Halford's third stepmother!

One day she asked Mrs Beazer how many gentlemen there were in the house.

'Only Mr Godwin and Mr La Trope. Why?'

'Well,' she said, 'I was wondering which one I could have to sleep with me tonight?'

Chapter 18

Miss Gordon had left and we now had a Miss Lake in the two front rooms on the drawing-room floor, and a Miss Scott in a bed-sitting-room on the next floor. Miss Scott's father had been an Indian judge and she was living on a pension and seemed to be really 'hard up'. When she heard the rag-and-bone man calling out, she would say, 'Oh go away. I eat my bones and wear my rags,' and poor dear, if she had not patched and mended they would be rags. She was making herself a pair of drawers and needed them so badly, that she would hem one leg and wear them, and the evening of the next day she would hem the other leg and put the lace on one and wear them again, and the next night finish them and start on the next pair! We liked her. She was no trouble and never grumbled if she was kept waiting for her food, and Albion used to keep her weekly bill as low as possible!

Peggy, the good girl who was there when we came, had now left and I had two new girls, both fourteen years old, Olive and Kate. Olive was upstairs girl. Such a cheerful girl and she always *looked* clean and tidy. She had lovely red hair that never seemed to get out of place, but to my horror, one day when I was helping her to make the beds, I saw five lice on her collar.

'Olive,' I said, 'did you know that you had lice?'

I said I would comb her hair that afternoon, so I let Kate go out for an hour, as I wanted to keep this from her as long as I could. I pulled down the kitchen blind, lit the gas and spread a large sheet of white drawer paper on the table. I had the shock of my life. Before I had the tooth comb through her hair, the lice were dropping down like rain. We could not kill them fast enough and I felt sick. Olive was crying, but I told her not to worry. I would comb her hair every day, but I would have to tell Kate and I would have to make her the upstairs maid, as I was afraid Olive would be dropping lice in the beds when we made them. Kate was very pleased to be 'upstairs' and Olive took it very well, but of course it made her unhappy.

Well, every afternoon I would comb her hair. Sometimes she would rebel and say she was not going to have it done, but she always let me and I really thought I was winning. Then she would go home for her half-day off, and come back full of lice again. At last I could not go on fighting and I most reluctantly told Olive she would have to leave. I never parted with a nicer girl, or one who looked nicer or cleaner! I gave her a good reference, but I did not mention the lice! She stayed in her next 'place' for seven years, when she married.

Chapter 19

The next maid was also named Olive. She was a fat, mucky little girl, but so willing and anxious to please. She and Kate stayed with me for more than two years! I was told that Mrs Garraway never seemed to keep a maid for more than a few months! It was a very 'hard' place with no modern conveniences. There were seven wash-stands, and the large jugs and small glass carafes had to be filled each day, and the girl had to carry the water from the kitchen. I worried about this, and I thought as there were two lavatories upstairs there must be water pipes somewhere, and looking round I saw a pipe in the corner on the landing on the first floor and there was one on the floor above. I told Albion about it and he called in Charlie Rich, and he fixed a tap on the two pipes at 5 shillings each. What a boon! And to think that Mrs Garraway had had the house for forty-one years, and all that time the girls had had to carry the heavy enamel jugs right up from the basement, seventy-nine stairs, to the top of the house!

Mrs Halford was then eighty-nine years old and had taken to her bed, and Mrs Beazer was looking after her.

I had a lady who had called several times and asked me if the old lady had gone and would I let her know as soon as she had, as she would like to take the rooms. She said she was Miss Grierson and that she had been living in Grosvenor for twenty-six years. I never heard how she came to hear of us, but I did think that paying £1,000 for the Good Will with only two sets of rooms let was taking advantage of us, but apparently Mrs Garraway's reputation was good. Well, Mrs Halford died at 4.20 on Christmas morning 1934. I had 'suffered' her for six years! A day or two before she died she sent for me and she said, 'You don't like me do you?'

I said, 'You have never given me cause to like you and plenty of cause to dislike you.'

'Yes, I know,' she said, 'I have been rather unkind to you, but now I am soon going to meet my Maker and I don't want you on my conscience so give your 'paw' and tell me you forgive me.'

As soon as the funeral was over, Miss Halford said she would not be able to afford the rooms without 'Madam' and that she had made arrangements to go into a home at Epsom kept by Church of England nuns. I was sorry to lose her; she was really good. She gave me a picture of herself when she was three years old and her mother died. She also gave me her silver backed brushes and comb – she said no one would keep them polished as I would!

I let Miss Grierson know that the rooms were vacant, and she came to see them and liked them. She asked if she could bring one or two pieces of her own furniture, also she would like the bedroom floor covered with linoleum and she would also like to have electricity! Up to now there was no electricity in the house and when I told Albion he was worried about the cost. We were very hard up. Arnold was still calling for his money every month, and every month we had to borrow another £100 at 6 per cent to get 'straight' as he called it. He never missed a chance to tell us it was due to me that we could not make ends meet!

Miss Grierson said she would pay half the cost! Of course I had not told her that we were financially embarrassed. So the men came and they had to dig up a bit of the road to connect us. Miss Grierson had two points in her sitting room, two in her bedroom and one in the spare room, and the complete bill was £8, That was in 1934.

Miss Grierson was a real gentlewoman. Her mother had been Lady-in-Waiting to Queen Charlotte and Miss Grierson's Christian name was Charlotte. She had one brother who was the Bishop of Durham and her brother, Sir George, was probably the world's greatest linguist. He is credited with understanding 300 languages and Indian dialects. (This I have quoted from an old newspaper cutting.)

Miss Grierson had one or two fads; one was that I did not cook any of her food in aluminium. This meant that I could not cook her potatoes in the pot with the others. This was about the only thing that I cooked for everyone, as all the other food was of their own choosing. Still, it was a very small price to pay for having such a lovely lady. She was eighty-one years old when she came to me and used to have one whole day a week in bed. Although the lavatory was only just across the hall, she used her chamber-pot when she had her day in bed. The pot had a lid made to fit it and if she used it for a 'motion' she would place a penny on the lid for the maid who emptied it! One day she said the little maid Olive was a bright willing girl, but could I train her to bring her a drink without spilling it in the saucer! So of course I had a chat with Olive and she said she would not spill it. Miss Grierson, who had a keen sense of humour, said Olive brought it to her and nearly pushed it into her face saying, 'Not a drop, not a drop!'

She liked to make her own coffee after dinner and at the side of the fireplace was a cupboard where she kept her pot and cups and saucers, etc. One day I lifted the pot down for her, and the spout was packed with beetles! I felt sick and ashamed, but all she said was, 'Oh dear, what a pest these are, it must be a great trial for you!' What a wonderful lady she was!

I was very happy with Miss Grierson on the hall floor, the two Miss Greaves in the drawing-room, and Miss Lake in the two front rooms; all nice considerate people, but we needed to let more rooms. So we got a Miss Scott in a bed-sitting-room and a Miss Talbot in the large back bedroom overlooking the park and glorious views beyond. I had a very busy time as I was now cooking five different dinners each day with only little Olive to help, and Albion who did the shopping and numerous repairs round the house because Mrs Garraway had certainly let the place fall into great disrepair. What a blessing it was that Albion was so clever with his hands; there did not seem to be a repair he could not tackle.

One day when I was in the drawing-room seeing the Miss Grieves about something, Miss Rose, the younger one, said, 'Mrs Godwin, my sister and I are so distressed to see you have a few lines coming on your face and you so young. We don't want you to get like us, so we have bought you some Elizabeth Arden's orange cream for night use. Will you please us by using it at night?' What darlings they were! I took it and thanked them very much. They little knew that I went to bed so tired, I could not do more than just wash my face and hands before getting into bed, where I dropped off to sleep as soon as my head touched the pillow. I nearly broke my heart when they said they were finding the hill up to the house and the stairs too much for them and they would have to leave. They had twenty-four stairs up to the drawing-room and another twenty-four to their bedroom and to the lavatory!

I never had to advertise my rooms and, soon after the darling Miss Grieves had left, two ladies called. They were both elderly and one had an old-fashioned ear trumpet! I thought, 'Its no good talking to her, I'll talk to the other one.' But the other one said, 'It's no good talking to me. I am stone deaf. Talk to my friend.' So I talked to the ear trumpet, a Miss Levine. The upshot was that Miss Kersey, the stone deaf lady, took the drawing-room floor, and I had her for nine years. She died during the war years.

My dear Miss Grierson had caught a bad cold and had taken to her bed, and her doctor had been to see her. He was Dr Harper and he visited her with a small dog under each arm! Miss Grierson thought the world of Dr Harper! Her cold had turned to pneumonia and I managed to get a woman to come in each night at 5 shillings a night. The doctor had been again and said, 'She won't last the night, but don't bother to call me, I'll call in the morning'!

I thought it was perfectly horrid of him to put it so casually. I wish I had sat up with her, but I had tonsillitis and my temperature was 102. I went in, in the morning, with tea for the woman and Miss Grierson was dead. The woman had been giving her brandy, but had let it run down in all the hollows in her neck, for she was a very thin lady. How I grieved over her death and the fact that I myself was really too ill to look after her. She died on Christmas Eve. The doctor came in the morning (without his dogs) and wrote out the death certificate, and told us to get in touch with her niece, the Bishop's daughter and her husband. We had a job, as they were travelling to visit friends. I had to leave all that to Albion and I hear they were located at a railway station!

A lady called and said she had been a friend of Miss Grierson and she would like to take her room. I did not 'take' to her at all, but I thought if she was a friend of Miss Grierson she must be nice. She was absolutely horrid and I had her for twelve years!

I never had time to go out in the daytime, so each evening when I had finished sending up the light suppers I would take our two dogs for a walk. I had to pass the (old) Eye Infirmary which was on a corner and was surrounded with shrubs. One evening, Nellie, the Jack Russell, was in among the shrubs and Don, the retriever, was sitting beside me. I was whistling for Nellie when a man with a rough haired terrier said, 'Excuse me, Mam, but your dog is sitting beside you.'

I said, 'Yes, I know he is, but I have a little one in the shrubs,' and just then Nellie appeared.

'Oh, I see,' said the man. 'Do you know, I thought you must be mad!' We both laughed and walked together to the Gravel Walk, Victoria Park. When I got in, I said, 'I've been walking with a man and his dog and he thought I must be mad.'

After that I would meet Harry each night and we would walk and talk together and I always told Albion.

One night he said, 'It's time I met this man of yours; bring him in tonight.' So I took Harry in and he and Albion had a friendly chat and a glass of cider. After he left, Albion said, 'I don't mind you meeting him; he is quite safe and so are you'!

Well, Harry became a dear and true friend to us, and in many ways, without actually telling me he loved me, I knew he did.

One evening he said, 'I have a little present for you.' And he gave me a gold sovereign and said, 'Like you, dear, pure gold.' I was very touched, but Harry was a good man, and he knew I was in love with my husband. He was a foreman upholsterer for a large store in Bath and he had been there fifty-one years when he retired. We thought he was not too well off. I saw him one evening and I asked him where he was going, and he said, 'Down to Walcot, beans are a halfpenny cheaper there!' When he died, two years after Albion, he left a considerable amount of money and eighteen houses, etc.

We had now been in the house for seven years. I told Albion that when Arnold came for his money this time he would offer us a different agreement.

'Oh, I don't see why he should,' said Albion.

'Well, he will,' I said, 'and I am coming in to see what he offers!'

So when Arnold came about 12.30, as he always did, I went in with Albion.

'What are you doing here?' said Arnold. 'Shouldn't you be doing your dinner?'

'No,' I said, 'I would like to hear what you have to say.'

'Well,' said Arnold, 'I do business with Mr. Godwin,' and turning to Albion he said, 'Now look here mister, we can't go on like we've been doing: me lending you £100 each month, all on account of your good lady not running the house the way I told her to, so I have drawn up a new Contract in which you will not become tenants with the option to buy at the end of fourteen years. Now just sign here, mister, and I'll be going.'

I said, 'That is preposterous! Don't sign that Albion.'

'Well what can we do?'

I said, 'If you sign that I will leave you, and you can run the house on your own.'

Arnold said, 'Don't listen to her. She wouldn't do that.'

I said, 'Albion – I would.'

He said again, 'Well, what can we do?'

I said, 'I don't know, but I know that Contract will not be signed.' I turned to Arnold and said, 'Come back in two weeks' time, after we have consulted a lawyer.' 'Oh, missus,' he said, 'you don't want to see no lawyer; you're dealing with a friend'.

I said, 'We will see a lawyer as we should have done in the first place. Now please go,' and he went.

'Oh, girl,' said Albion, 'what are we going to do?'

'Well, we will see a lawyer. I will ask Miss Grieson if she can recommend one. She has lived in Bath twenty-six years.'

I told Miss Grieson we needed to see a lawyer and she told us to whom to go. So we went to this old established firm and saw the 'Head'. He read our past Contract and said, 'Please excuse me, but you are two of the most trusting fools I have ever met!'

He told us we must get out of this man's hands at once. He said, 'Have you anyone who would lend you £1,000 or two.

I said, 'No', but Albion said his brother could, but he did not like to ask him.

'Well, I will,' said the lawyer. 'Give me his phone number and I'll get on to him right away.'

He did and Eustace came down the next day, and we all met in the lawyer's office. He, the lawyer, got us a £1,000 mortgage and Eustace lent us £1,000 and we never saw Arnold again! It was wonderful – two pests gone – Arnold and the beetles! I felt as if a weight had been lifted from me.

Chapter 20

I, of course, had two different maids now – Violet and Mabel. Mabel only stayed about 18 months, but Violet stayed for five years and she loved us and we her. She came from Wales as most of my girls did. Her father was a butcher and her mother was dead. I think she could not have been too happy with her father as she almost looked on Albion and me as mother and father. She was a very good maid and so we allowed her a lot of privileges. She loved dancing and would go to any at the Western Hotel and at Christ Church Hall. Sometimes, when it was not her evening off, there would be a dance and she would ask to go. It meant that I would have to take up the hot water and turn down the beds. 'But I will make it up to you, madam,' she would say, and she did! At about this time I was going each morning to the doctor to have my eye probed as I had a blocked tear duct. It was a very painful 'operation' and I would walk home through the park and up our garden, and Violet would watch for me coming and bring me in, sit me down, and get me a cup of tea.

'Now you rest for half an hour,' she would say, 'and don't worry. I have set Mabel doing the vegetables. There is plenty of time for you to have a little rest and recover.'

I have sat up till two in the morning making her a new dance dress, and I once made her a Guard's uniform for a fancy dress dance. When she was 18 years old she said she would like to 'better herself.'

'What did you think of doing?' I asked.

'Well, I thought I would like to be a "nippy".' A nippy was a waitress at one of Lyons Corner houses, very popular cafés in those days; alas, now they are all gone.

I said, 'I cannot think you will be bettering yourself as a nippy, but if that is what you would like to do, go and have a try, and if you do not like it you can always come back to us. You will have to learn to carry the try on one hand shoulder high.'

Why did I have to tell her that! Albion and I were sitting reading on a Sunday afternoon when there was a terrible crash. Violet had been trying to carry the tray nippy fashion, and there down the stairs and against the wall was butter and jam, milk, sugar and tea. What a mess! and Violet sitting on the stairs. Every bit of china was broken, and in those days it was good china and everything matched.

'I am not going to try to be a nippy,' she said.

A while later she said she would like to train to be a nurse. 'Good,' I said, 'that will be "bettering" yourself.'

So Violet started writing to matrons of London hospitals, but alas, the letters were badly written and Violet was getting, as she put it, 'Fed up, madam.'

She said, 'Will you write the letters for me?'

'No, Violet, I am sure they must be your own letters.'

I suggested to her that she tried getting into a mental hospital, and the first one she wrote to asked for an interview. So I went with her to Epsom and we had to report to the porter. He was in a little place halfway up the drive. He directed us where to go. Violet clutched my arm.

'Madam,' she said, 'did you see inside his room there. Every key had a whistle attached.'

'What a good idea,' I said. 'It must give one a lovely feeling of safety to know one has only to whistle and help would come.'

By now we had reached the main entrance and the door was opened to us, and locked again as soon as we were in. Presently a Sister came in another door which she had had to unlock, and she locked it again as soon as she was in!

She asked Violet a few questions, and said, 'I think you will do. When can you start? Can you stay now?'

'Oh no,' said Violet, 'I haven't got my clothes with me!'

'But you have your night-dress and toothbrush so you could stay.' I said.

'Right then,' said the Sister. 'Say goodbye to your friend and come with me.'

'But madam,' said Violet in a real panic, 'I don't think this is what I want.'

I said to the Sister, 'Could she come on a month's trial? If she doesn't like it and she doesn't suit you, she can come back to us.'

'Yes, all right, but now say your goodbyes and come along.'

Poor Violet clung to me and I tried to cheer her up. Did she not know how I was going to miss her? She stayed there for four years and went from there to St Mary's Hospital, Paddington where she stayed until she became a Ward Sister and then a Health Visitor. We were very proud of her. Then she married her 'Standing Dish' as she called him, a young man from her home town whom she had known since their school days – a funny expression, which I had never heard before and I have never heard it since. She had had many sweethearts, but she always said, 'I expect in the end I shall marry my Standing Dish.' Two years later we had a letter from him in which he said, 'I know that you will be grieved to hear that our beloved Violet died in childbirth.' We were heartbroken for we had loved her like a daughter.

I had a very good maid for over four years; she came straight from school. Her name was Mary; the other girl was Alice and had been with me for just over a year. Upstairs I had Mrs Babington and her maid on the hall floor, Miss Kersey, the deaf lady and her companion, a Miss Fern, a clergyman's daughter (one among many). I had a charming Miss Cave and her friend on the next floor, and in the top room, a Miss Talbot. She came with her mother who was a short motherly looking lady, but was as hard as nails! Her daughter was tall and thin and very pleasant looking. The mother said, 'I want the room for my daughter and I would like you to just keep an eye on her. She sometimes gets very depressed. She has some bromide with her; just give her a dose when she needs it. You will find she is no trouble.' She did not seem to be any trouble, but one or two things seemed a bit funny. For instance her room was 24 feet by 18 feet and she would have her 3 foot bed right bang in the middle of the room. It looked most queer.

One day Mary came to me and said, 'Madam, I wish you would go up and see Miss Talbot; she is acting a bit funny.' There was Miss Talbot dancing round the room with nothing on but a short vest and she was blowing a tin whistle! I smiled and said, 'What are you doing, dear?'

She said, 'I'm a nymph, I'm a fairy.'

I said, 'You will catch cold if you don't put more clothes on.'

'On no,' she said, 'fairies never catch cold.'

After a while I got her into bed and she started to cry and sob, and I petted her up a bit. She clung to me and said that I was like the dearest mother in the world to her. She was two years older than me!

Chapter 21

It was 1939 and the Second World War had started. Many people had Anderson shelters in their gardens, but Albion was against that. He said the safest place would be our basement kitchen, and that there was no reasons to suppose the Germans would drop bombs on Bath, but my word they *did*!

The war helped me a bit because I now had all the ration books and for the first time in eleven years I cooked the same meals for all of us.

I asked Mrs Talbot to take her daughter away as the top rooms in the house were not nice to be in and I was sorry for the poor thing as she seemed to have a most unsympathetic mother.

Albion had joined the Home Guard and he was away most nights. When the air raid warning went I had to force myself to get out of bed to look after the old ladies. We banked up the kitchen range and kept the big kettle going for the comforting 'cuppas.'

It was 1942 and Bath was bombed! There were two nights of fierce and unexpected bombing. We had 401 dead and over 200 houses destroyed. We had a bomb in the garden; a split second more and it would have been on the house. It dropped in the garden 3 yards from the house and a piece of shrapnel came right through the small bedroom and lodged in the wall in the inner hall, and on the other side of the wall was Mrs Babington's bed! She never knew how close to death she, and in fact all of us, were that night. I was busy looking after the five ladies in the kitchen, and then dashing up to the hall bedroom to make sure Mrs Babington was all right.

'Of course I am all right,' she snapped. 'If I am going to die I'll die in my bed. Go and look after those silly women downstairs.'

It was as I reached the bottom stair that I saw the policeman.

'My, you gave me a fright,' I said. 'What is the matter?'

'Don't you know that you have a light at the top of the house?'

'Oh, no,' I said, 'I'll run up and turn if off at once.'

'I'll come with you,' he said. We toiled up the sixty-nine stairs into the top back room and there, sure enough, the centre light was on! The window had been blown out and strips of wood were nailed across, but of course between the slits the light shone through and could be seen for miles! The policeman wanted to know whose room it was and many details.

'Are you in this big house alone?' he asked.

'Oh no,' I said, 'I have one old lady in bed on the hall floor and five more in the basement kitchen.'

'Have you a husband?' he asked.

'Yes,' I said, 'but he is away being a Home Guard.'

'Well,' he said, 'I suppose you know you've had a bomb in the garden?'

'What!' I said. 'A bomb in the garden!'

'Yes,' he said, 'come and look.' And there almost up to the French doors was this great crater!

'I'll get the men in in the morning to make sure it is safe.' It must have been a 500 lb. one and a split second later it would have come on the house.

I was definitely shaken, but he told me he was sure we would be safe for the rest of the night.

I said, 'I must get back to my old ladies or they will be so worried, but I won't mention about the bomb to them.'

He said, 'Good-night,' and left. I went into the kitchen and I had to laugh because they were all covered in soot! The bomb must have caused the soot to come down the chimney. What a mess! I quickly washed down the table and then I made a fresh pot of tea. I felt safe as I felt sure the bomber would not come again that night.

I had only the one maid, Mary, and she helped to clean up the mess. Mrs Babington never knew how near she came to dying that night! A piece of shrapnel had come right through the small bedroom and lodged in the wall in the hall just above her bed on the other side! We only had the two nights of this reprisal bombing, but in those two nights 917 died, more than 200 historic buildings were destroyed and several of our beautiful old churches. The sirens were sounded 519 times in Bath.

Mrs Kersey, my deaf lady, died at the beginning of the war. She would not have heard a bomb or a siren. She was eighty-four. She left me all her clothes! Her cousin was distressed that she had not left me any money, but I had not expected any! The cousin who was disposing of her personal things asked if I could spare any combinations or petticoats for Miss Kersey's companion, Miss Fern, as she had not been left anything at all! I said she could have everything as I was sure there was nothing of any use to me. I did not wear combinations!

Chapter 22

I now had only Mrs Cave and Mrs Babington and just the one maid. I said to Albion, 'We must let more rooms, as we are still in the red, but with all the will in the world I cannot run this house without maids and Mary is longing to go and do war work, and it will be impossible to get other maids.'

'Well what can we do?' said Albion.

'We can turn it into flats,' I said.

'Tell me what you want done,' said Albion, 'and I will do everything except the plumbing, and we can get Rich in to do that.'

We had the three good rooms on each floor. The smallest was 16 feet by 14, so I told Albion we need not touch the two large rooms: one would be a double bedroom and one a drawing-room. The other could be partitioned and made into a kitchen and bathroom.

Mrs Babington had had a woman to help her. At first they came by day, but later they lived in. In the nine years she was with me she had had ten different women. Some would stay a couple of weeks, some a week, and one stayed only one night. I wrote to her people and said I could not get anyone else for her, and the only way I could keep her was to have her in our bedroom, and we would put our bed in our sitting-room. This they readily agreed to, so we got her down, and after May and I had thoroughly cleaned her rooms, we moved Miss Cave into them – which pleased her very much as she was nearly eighty-four and was finding the stairs a great trial. We soon had the drawing-room floor converted into a flat and the only things we had to buy for it were cleaning materials, i.e., brooms and brushes, etc. It was let almost immediately as the Admiralty had moved from London to

Bath and the people were clamouring for accommodation.

I had been letting that floor for £2.12s.6d. per week, and for this I had to do all the cooking and keep the rooms clean, and also bed and table linen. Now I let the floor for £3 a week and nothing to do for them.

Albion soon had Miss Cave's old rooms ready and that too was quickly let, as was the top floor. Mary had now left. She had been with me for six years and was a treasure, and we parted with sadness.

I had a great trial in Mrs Babington. She was now bedridden, filthy in her habits: she would spit her phlegm onto the sheet or into the glass of water! We had a bell which she could press in her bed, and yet she would do her motions in the bed and ring when she had done them. Oh the filthy draw sheets that I had to wash, and the horrible phlegm, filthy woman, and a very horrid one too. It was a great relief when she died at ninety-two. Her relations came and took her away (she had no children) and the chief niece said, 'Mrs Godwin we are each going to give you £1 for being so good to auntie; that will be £20. I will give you the addresses of those who are not here so that you can write to each one and thank them for the £1'!

What a wonderful, wonderful relief it was when Mrs Babington died. I quickly cleaned the room and was so happy to move back into it because, of course, we had not enjoyed having our bed in the sitting-room.

I now had only Miss Cave to look after and she was really no trouble until she started to go a bit funny in the head! I woke up one night hearing a noise in the hall above.

'Albion,' I said, 'there is someone moving about in the hall.' And while I was telling him I was putting on my dressing-gown and shoes.

'All right,' said Albion, 'I'll go and see.'

I went up and there was Miss Cave holding a stone hot water-bottle (we could not get rubber ones during the war) and walking about.

'Did you want something, dear?' I asked.

'Well, yes,' she said. 'I was looking for a ladder to take me to Heaven.'

'Well, dear,' I said, 'it is ten minutes to two o'clock and even St Peter has to rest sometimes, so I'm sure you would not be able to get in until the morning, so come back to bed now.'

So she came back to bed and I refilled her bottle and made her a cup of tea, and within half an hour she was asleep. I took her her tea and a jug of hot water to wash with at 8 o'clock next morning. Now I am a great believer in prayer and I asked to be guided as to whether to tell her or not. I said, 'Good morning, Miss Cave, did you sleep well?'

'No,' she said, 'I did not. I have a feeling that I left my bed in the night.'

So I told her and she laughed. 'Oh dear,' she said, 'that was rather a silly thing to do. I might have fallen down into the well.'

I said, 'You were going up to Heaven, not to Hell, and I cannot put tables to stop you going up or falling down. Would you like me to put a camp-bed in your room and sleep there?'

'Oh, that would be nice,' she said.

So Albion brought up the camp-bed and when I found her getting out of bed, which she did most nights, I would persuade her to get back and I would make a pot of tea. There was a gas ring on the hearth and I always took up a tray ready, and after a cup of tea she would settle down and be asleep within 15 minutes. Then I would get my own much needed rest. Miss Cave had two friends who visited her quite often. They were sisters – Miss Humphrey, who was a retired nursing sister, and Mrs Humphrey Jones, whose deceased husband had been chauffeur to Queen Mary. They would sit, one either side of her, holding her hands and calling her sweet names, but when she developed a cold they would not come near her. They would phone up and ask how she was, and I would tell them. Then Mrs Jones would say, 'Give her our dearest love and we hope she will soon be better.'

I said, 'I am sure she would appreciate a visit from you.'

'Yes, Mrs Godwin, I'm sure she would but we dare not risk catching a cold. You see there is only my sister and I to look after each other.'

I said, 'I am looking after her and running the house!'

Anyway Miss Cave got rather queer in the head. She said she had a little boy of eight years old under the bed, and he was too shy to come out! She said, 'If I were to pour some tea in the saucer, you call him out and I will give it to him.' So she said, 'Come along, dear, don't be shy. Mrs Godwin has some nice tea for you.'

I nursed her night and day. Her doctor was Dr Linsay and I asked him if he would like her to have a trained nurse. He said, 'My dear, no one would or could look after her better than you. What a loss you are to the profession.' I think that was one of the nicest compliments ever paid to me.

Chapter 23

At this time I was receiving letters from my sister Annie telling me that our mother was dying and demanding me to come home and look after her. 'I cannot leave her alone,' she said, 'and I am having to pay a housekeeper to look after her and the apartment, and I cannot really afford it, so you must come home. It is your duty.'

Well, I had no maids now and I could not leave Miss Cave, also one could not travel across the sea without a permit. Thinking about it since, I owed nothing to my mother or my sister. I had kept myself entirely since I was fourteen years old. The letters between us were few and far between. I had had a brooch from my mother and a similar one from Annie on my twenty-first birthday, and for my wedding present my mother gave me a crochet bag in which to keep my brush and comb, and Annie gave me a tray cloth! So I was certainly under no obligation to either of them.

However, Albion kindly made enquiries from the shipping people. Miss Cave died peacefully and I did all that was necessary for her, and her brothers came and arranged about the funeral. She had not been buried two days when I got a letter from the Shipping Company telling me to send a cheque for £56 and go to Leith where a boat would be waiting to take me to Canada. In her will she left £200 to each of the two sisters and any pieces of furniture that was hers, for although our rooms were fully furnished we always let anyone bring any special or favourite piece of furniture with them. Miss Cave's brother (the retired schoolmaster) wrote to me and said he was vexed that 'those vultures' had got the better of her in the end, and he was grieved I was not mentioned after all I had done for his sister. He said he was the poorest of the family, but would I please accept the enclosed £50 as a mark of his gratitude!

The boat I went on to Canada was a freighter and took only ten passengers. There was a bumptious man who was an envoy in New York. There was Ben Spoor MP, and a Canadian newsreader on the television who shared a cabin with the Canon Fry, who said it was like living in a bar as the Canadian was a great drinker. There was a most charming Polish Countess who shared a cabin with Elizabeth, a retired teacher. I shared a cabin with a young Canadian girl who had married an Englishman, and he was going to follow her as soon as he could get permission to go to Canada. We all shared the Captain's table and were always all seated when the Captain came in. I was right opposite the door and he always winked at me!

I said to Elizabeth, 'The Captain always winks at me when he comes in.'

She said, 'Well, you always wink at him.'

I had no idea that I did! One night I was returning from the bathroom; it was 2.45 and I met the Captain.

'Oh hello,' he said, 'come into my cabin; I want to show you something.'

So we went in together and he took me to the porthole and pointed out the icebergs.

'Did you not know we were stationary?' he asked.

'No,' I said.

'Well, of course, I can't move with those there,' he said.

Then we sat and talked and he showed me photos of his family and offered me a sherry, but I told him I did not drink. Next morning at breakfast, the First Officer said, 'She went in like a lamb to the slaughter.' I wonder what he meant?

I had only been in Montreal ten days when I had a cable to say my husband was taken ill and I was to return at once. 'Of course you can't go,' said Annie. 'Your duty is here with our mother.'

I said, 'Annie, my duty is with my husband.'

I phoned to his doctor, dear Dr Linsay, and he said he had had a heart attack and was better, and getting spoiled with all the attention he was receiving from the ladies in the flats. So my mind was at ease. My sister said she expected that he was just bereft! I landed on our twenty-fifth wedding anniversary. I had not planned to be away from Albion on that special day.

I have often wondered if my mother liked me. When I was betwen eight and fourteen and we lived together (except for the year she left me at the hotel!) we seemed close and she would confide in me. I would sit and sew with her and she would say I was like a right hand to her, but when I went to live with the Baileys when I was fourteen years old, I don't think I had more than two letters a year, one for my birthday and one for Christmas! Then, of course, there was the time when I was eighteen years old and she and Annie had been planning for months to emigrate to Canada and never said a word to me! She left and did not seem to be a bit concerned about me. I had my dear, friend, Jessie, who was about forty years older than me, and my mother said to her, 'I know she will be safe in your care'!

I was home three months before my mother died. She did not stay in bed. In fact it was a job to keep her in bed at night! Annie would sit up with her Friday night and Saturday night and I would hear her scolding mother saying, 'Stay in bed. You shall not get up even if I have to sit on your knees.'

I sat up with her from Sunday night till Friday and she would soon start pushing the bed clothes off and getting out. I would say, 'Where do you want to go?'

She would say, 'I would like to sit in the kitchen.' So we would sit together and chat and she would sometimes quietly sing her old song 'Ye Banks and Brays'.

One night she said, 'I want my daughter.'

I said, 'I am a daughter; will I do?'

'Not you, you silly little thing, I want my intelligent daughter.'

I know she was old and getting near the end, but it hurt. After she died on 24 November my sister's manner to me was quite different. She had always been really unkind and now she was sweetness itself. She said, strictly speaking, being in mourning she should not go out to dinner, etc., but she had had so many invitations because of me that she decided to accept them. So nearly every night we went to her friends for dinner and we gave one or two dinners to invite people back. Her friends were very kind and loaded me up with all sorts of good things – groceries which we were unable to get in England. (Rationing went on until 1954.)

When the six months permit was up I had orders to go to New York and board the *Queen Elizabeth*. (The fare was £68.) I had never been to New York and I was loaded with extra packages because of the kindness of Annie's friends. I thought she might have got a day off to take me to New York, but she never suggested it and neither did I. When I got to New York I found all the ladies were wearing their shoes and I had on my big boots. So I went into a doorway and changed, but a couple of hours later it started to snow heavily, so I changed back into my boots.

The four days on the *Queen Elizabeth* were lovely. I had my hair done and the hairdresser asked if I would like a henna rinse. I had never had a henna rinse, so I agreed and it brought out all the 'red' lights in my hair.

When I got home and Albion saw it, he said, 'Your hair looks lovely. I think the Canadian climate must suit you.' I never told him about the rinse which, of course, washed out with the next shampoo.

We docked at Southampton and we had to stay the night, so we booked into the Polygon Hotel, and I was shocked when I asked for a piece of bread with my dinner and the waiter said, 'If you have bread, madam, you can't have pudding'! I did not remember how rationed we were in England. I had come from a land of plenty.

As soon as I was settled in, I gave a dinner party and invited all the people in the house (ten of them) as a thank-you for their kindness to Albion after he had his heart attack. I was able to put a gift beside each plate, such as 1 lb. of sultanas, or sugar or suet. They were very pleased.

Chapter 24

As soon as I got home, my friends who had taken the hall floor flat for six months, left and I ordered a pale green Wilton carpet with the money Mr Cave had given me. Albion said, 'We must get the hall floor flat let; we can't afford to have it empty.'

I said, 'Well actually, it is let.'

'To whom?' asked Albion.

I said, 'To us.'

He said, 'Oh, I am not going up there. I like it down here. We have French doors to the garden and I have my little workshop.' (The conservatory really.)

I said, 'Well dear, I am going up there. We have been down here for eighteen years and I am sick of scrubbing these stone floors, and without maids I really cannot cope with all the work.' So I put the carpet down and carried up furniture. Albion did not help me, but he said, 'I hope you will leave me a table, a chair and an odd saucepan.'

When I had got the flat more or less ready I asked him if he would like to see it.

'My word, girl,' he said, 'it does look nice. Could you do with a lodger?'

We both laughed and he said, 'I'm sorry I have been so silly. I do hope you have not strained yourself carrying all this furniture up.'

Well, we brought the rest of the things up and in less than a week I had the garden flat let. Albion loved it on the hall floor. There were lovely views from the back windows, and in those days the countryside was not built upon and there were cows grazing. Albion, looking through his spyglass, said he could see the canal and the trains. By now we were getting on fairly well with all the flats let. We had not been able to afford to install cooking stoves, so I cooked for all of them and they willingly had whatever I could get. For as I said, the rationing went on till 1954, although gradually it became easier to get some things. As we could afford it, we would buy a gas or an electric cooker, and if a flat became vacant we would get an electrician or gas man to put it in. So by about 1958 all the flats were fitted up so that I did not need to do anything for them.

Albion, who had never grumbled about leaving the country and farm life, now said, 'One day, my love, we will get back to the country.'

I said, 'How could we do that?' and he said that we would buy a cottage. I asked how were we going to be able to go round looking for, and at, cottages as we had no car. He said he had noticed that the man who had taken the newsagents shop two doors away seemed to be a retired gentleman, but it looked as if he took people out in his car, so he would go and have a chat with him.

He did and Mr Wilson said he would be very pleased to run us round any time. So we looked through the *Bath Chronicle* and marked one or two cottages for sale and arranged to go and see them. We went to the car and there in the front seat was his wife.

'What's she doing here?' whispered Albion.

'Oh, I expect he is going to drop her somewhere,' I said. But he did not, and every time we went to look at cottages she came too. Albion was most annoyed.

'Doesn't she realise that this is a business arrangement?' he said.

I said, 'Well, why don't you speak to him about it?'

Albion said, 'Well, I should tell her, but I can't because we are bound to do business with them and we can't start off with a row.'

So he said nothing, and every time we went looking at cottages 'Mother came too'.

At last we saw one; well, actually it was two cottages together and, although they had not been fully converted into one, they went as one. Downstairs one could go right through, but one had to use both staircases to get to the upstairs rooms. Mrs Wilson told me that the cottage was being sold by auction at Bristol.

So we went and a man had just made a bid of £400, which the auctioneer had accepted when the man suddenly said, 'Hey, wait a bit, what's going to be done about all those trees in the meadows opposite? Going down the lane is like going into the Black Hole of Calcutta.'

'I don't know anything about the trees,' said the auctioneer. 'You would have to get in touch with the gentleman who bought the big house privately and in whose meadows the trees are.'

'Oh well, in that case,' said the man, 'I withdraw.'

So the somewhat exasperated auctioneer said, 'Now who will give me an advance on £400?'

Mrs Wilson gave me a nudge and said, 'Go on, bid.'

So I timidly said, '£450.'

'I am not taking fifties,' he said.

So I said, '£500' and the cottages were knocked down to me!

'Well, thank you ladies and gentlemen, that ends the sale.' To me he said, 'Come and let me have your cheque.'

I said, 'I haven't got a cheque.'

'Well,' he said, 'cash will do.'

I said, 'I am sorry, but I haven't got any cash.'

He was furious. 'Have you just come to have an afternoon's fun? God knows what I can do now.'

I felt dreadful and really sorry for him.

'Please don't worry,' I said. 'You will have the cheque by the first post tomorrow.' (In 1959 one could post a letter in the evening and it would be delivered in the morning.)

'I must try and get it today,' he said. 'What is your phone number?'

'That's right,' I said. 'You phone my husband and he will assure you it is all right.'

Well, the poor man rang and rang and got no answer. I could not understand it as I knew Albion would be there.

'I will phone your bank,' he said.

'Well they won't tell you anything,' I said, and of course they did not.

'Who is your solicitor?' he asked.

I told him. 'But,' I said, 'we have not had to see him for seventeen years so I doubt if he would remember me.'

The poor man was in a terrible state and he asked Mrs Wilson if she would lend me the money (£50).

'I would in a minute,' she said, 'only I have not brought my cheque book with me.' (I have now known her for over forty years, and I have never known her not to have her cheque book with her!)

'Please try not to worry,' I told the auctioneer. 'I promise you, you will have my husband's cheque in the morning.' He raved a bit and I felt pretty awful, but there was nothing to do but leave it.

I got outside and went to the nearest phone and called Albion. I told him what had happened and asked him to go at once and post a cheque for £50 to the auctioneer, which he did and the poor man of course got it the next morning. He even wrote to me to apologise for 'going for me' so much, but of course he was quite justified.

Albion was very pleased I had brought the cottages. They were solidly made with stone and there was a good slate roof. Inside it was quite dilapidated, but there was nothing we could not tackle ourselves. Each cottage contained a sitting room 17 ft. 6 in. by 13 ft. 6 in. Upstairs there were two landings 16 ft. by 8 ft. and two small bedrooms in each cottage. 'Could you knock the wall down between the two small bedrooms?' I asked. Albion said if they were lath and plaster he could, and he did. So now we had two good sized rooms downstairs and the same up, in addition to the two large landings. Each cottage had a small kitchen where there was a copper and a bread oven. There was no water laid on, but a good well which had never been known to run dry. And of course, there was a bucket in an outside privy. We bought an Elsan toilet, which I in my ignorance thought emptied itself somehow! There was a large garden, less than one quarter acre. It had been dug up all over except for a cluster of blackcurrant bushes.

We moved in towards the end of July and Albion quickly planted a few vegetables, but we had to work on the cottages and there was a lot to do. We both enjoyed working on them. The village was at Wick, only 8 miles from Bath, with a bus service four times a day at 1s.6d. return!

The very nice man who had driven us round (with his wife) came out, and was always glad to help. He was one of the nicest men I have ever met.

The lane was a cul-de-sac leading into fields on the left, and on the right was a drive leading to the big house, which had been bought by a consultant doctor who worked in Bristol, which also was about eight miles away. There were four children aged from nineteen months to fourteen years.

We spent a very happy time doing repairs to the cottage. I would go into Bath each Saturday to collect the rents from the five flats. Each tenant would put his rent book with cheque inside, on the hall table and I would just sign each book and leave it on the table. If anyone wanted to see me they knew I would come in on the twenty-past-ten bus and would be looking out for me. Quite often someone would be looking for me just to have a little chat. The flats were all let furnished, so if and when anyone left I would have to come in and clean the flats, and replace anything, but there were not many changes.

When it got near Christmas, Albion said, 'Ducky, do you think we could give a little party for the doctor's children. You know they are fresh here, like us and won't know anyone in the village?'

I said, 'Of course we could.' So I ran down the drive and saw Mrs Hughes and told her what we would like to do, and she said she was sure they would be delighted to come (and they were!) We sent them a little note asking for the pleasure of their company for tea on Boxing Day.

On 5 November it was a beautiful day, quite mild for the time of the year and Albion was in the garden trimming a hedge. He came in laughing and said, 'Ducky, me fall down in the ditch. I had hold of what I thought was a big branch to cut it off, and it was loose and I went backwards into the ditch.'

'Did you hurt yourself?' I asked.

'Oh no,' he said, 'but I have had a little lump here,' putting his hand on his tummy, 'and it seems to have brought it out. Feel.' I felt and was shocked. He had a lump like a small ball!

'How long have you had this?' I asked.

'Oh, a long time, but it doesn't hurt and never seemed to get any bigger until I fell.'

'Well,' I said, 'I am going to fetch the doctor to you.'

We had only been in the cottage for four months so had not registered with the doctor, but when I told him about the lump he said, 'Why did not you and your husband come to the surgery?'

I said, 'Well you do live rather a long way from us and he is in his eightieth year.'

The doctor was very sorry and I think eighty seemed a great age to him. He said he would come that afternoon, which he did. He gave Albion a very thorough examination and when I took him into the kitchen to wash his hands, he said, 'Mrs Godwin, your husband has a growth and it is so gross that nothing can be done. I am afraid his days are numbered.'

I could not believe I was hearing right. 'When you say numbered, how long do you mean?'

'Oh, four and half to five months,' he said. 'When you go in there, act naturally and don't let him know that he has cancer. I won't come again until he starts getting the pains and then you must send for me.'

'But can't you operate or treat him in some way?'

'No,' he said. 'I have not found the primary, but the secondary is in the liver and we have not started liver transplants yet, though even that will come in time.'

He said a cheery goodbye to Albion, and I went back to him and I could have fallen on his shoulder and wept. Instead I said, 'Well, there is not too much wrong with you because the doctor is not coming again unless we send for him.'

Albion was so thrilled with the wonderful examination the doctor had given him. He did not seem concerned about the result.

'Do you know, girl,' he said. 'I have never had an examination before!'

So we had been married for thirty-four years and except that he once had erysipelas, he had wonderful health. He had never had a headache and he said he was never tired, which amazed me as I was never not tired. I had told the doctor what a lot of work we had to do on the cottages and I said, 'I must stop him now.'

'Oh no,' he said. 'Let him do whatever he wants to, nothing will make any difference.'

So we worked away together and I tried never to let him know how sad I felt. I made a great effort with the children's party knowing it was going to be our last Christmas together. Albion loved children and had 'picked up' at auction sales various toys. We had several mechanical toys and we had a pintable. With a Vim carton Albion inserted a small spiral spring, which he held down with string, which was put through a hole in the bottom and made secure with seal-wax. Then we filled the carton with all sorts of small gifts. Albion had said, 'Get nice things, girl; we can't give the doctor's children cheap rubbish.' So I bought one or two little animals that looked like alabaster, a silver thimble, a few silver coins, and several gold wrapped chocolates. The top was covered with a piece of tissue paper.

On the afternoon after tea, it was stood on a small tin with methylene which Albion lighted. It melted the sealing wax and up popped the spring, sending all the little gifts all over the floor. It was a great success and the two boys John and George were delighted to scramble around picking them up. We also had a present for each one off the beautifully decorated tree. For the little eighteen-month-old girl Janet, I had a small doll and I had dressed her in a really lovely cotton crocheted dress. There were, of course, lots of good things to eat. About eight o'clock Willimina, who was fourteen years old, said it was time they went home. So after a hug from the boy and a kiss from the girls we watched them down their drive.

The next day we had a note from the three elder ones. George who was eight years old wrote, 'Dear Mr and Mrs Godwin, Thank you for the party you gave us. It was the most beautiful old fashioned party I have ever been to and I and all of us enjoyed it very much.'

As soon as Christmas was over, Albion said we must get on to work and asked, 'What would you like me to do, love?'

'Well if you would fill in the cracks in the ceiling in our bedroom I will come up as soon as I have put the stew on and colour washed the ceiling.'

So up he went and I got the vegetables peeled ready for the stew, when down came Albion.

'Oh, my dear,' he said, 'I am so sorry, I can't do it. I feel so ill.'

My heart sank as I knew this was the beginning of the end.

'Poor dear,' I said, 'I am sorry, but don't worry about the work. We have got all the time in the world in which to do it. You must come and sit in your nice new chair I gave you for Christmas, and I will get the doctor to come and have a look at you.'

He never did any more work, but got weaker every day. He suffered a great deal of pain and had to have injections to kill it. He did not take to his bed for another month and then I got it downstairs in the sitting-room. I put it by the window so he had a view of the garden. I asked him if he would like me to bring the little camp-bed and sleep downstairs with him, but he said, 'No, my love. I am all right. You get a good night's sleep.' But I didn't sleep and kept creeping down to see if he was all right. So I just brought the little bed down and slept beside him and he said, 'It is lovely to have you near.'

I said, 'You old silly, I have been longing to be with you!' He was a lovely patient and I loved nursing.

Sometimes he would say, 'Don't do any work, bring your knitting and sit beside me.' I was making a bedspread with different coloured hexagons. He would ask to see what colours I had knitted and he once said, 'Girl, you won't put this away when I am gone and not finish it?'

We had never discussed his illness and I was shocked when he said that. I knew then that he knew he was dying, so I did not say, 'Don't talk like that, you will live to see it done.' I just said, 'Of course I will finish it. I never leave a thing half done.' But it was fifteen years before I finished it. I would get it out, burst into tears and put it away.

He was preparing himself for his death. He said he would like me to ask Eustace (his favourite brother) to come and see him. Eustace came and I left them to have a quiet talk together. We had only been in the village a few months so had not made any friends, but the post-lady would take messages and the milkman would do any shopping in the village, and it was a village where one could buy all that one needed. I had asked Mr Askew who had been our tenant for a number of years if he would attend to the rents and bank the money. This he did and he did it most professionally. So I did not leave Albion at all for the last two months.

One day he asked me to get our friend Harry to come. Harry had, of course, been coming over each week, but sometimes Albion was not well enough to receive him. But when he came this time I took him in and Albion was not in too much pain. He took hold of both our hands and said,

'Harry, I know you love my girl very much, so I want you to look after her when I am gone: see she does not overdraw the bank and see that people don't take advantage of her. She is such an old silly.' Harry seemed embarrassed when Albion said he knew he loved me and Albion said, 'Don't worry, Harry, I always knew I could trust you both. I never worried.'

The two staircases at the cottage were horrid, very steep, and Albion would go first and say, 'Give me your hand, you poor old woman, I'll help you up.' When he was dying he said, 'Dear, the first thing you must have done when I'm gone is a new staircase. I'll never rest in my grave if I thought you were struggling up those stairs without me to help you.' It was the middle of March and he was in terrible pain and begged for an injection. So the doctor came and said, 'I cannot give you this injection without Mrs Godwin's consent.'

Albion said, 'Don't hesitate my love for I cannot stand any more pain.' So the doctor gave it and then took me aside and said I must have a friend with me that night. I said, 'I quite understand he will die tonight, but I like being with him and I will be quite all right.'

But he said, 'Please, to please me, have a friend with you.'

So I said, 'Well, the Wilsons will be coming out presently so I will see what they say.'

What Mrs Wilson said was, 'We will go and fetch Vera; she will say with you.'

Vera was a waitress and had her own house to look after. The manageress lived with her and was waited on by Vera hand, foot and finger. The Wilsons were free; why could they not have stayed? Well, they went to Vera and the poor dear was hoovering her sitting-room. Mr Wilson said if she would leave that he would run her out to me as there was no bus until 8.20. So the dear thing left her work, put a few things in a case and came out. What a wonderful friend she was (and is). We sat and chatted and had our supper. Albion was in a coma. I saw Vera upstairs to bed and sat down by Albion. I was glad he was out of pain. It was very quiet and peaceful. He did not come out of the coma but passed away at 1.30 on Saturday morning. I kissed him and stayed with him for an hour before calling Vera. I said I will have to wash him and put on clean pyjamas. I said, 'Do you mind helping me?'

'Of course not,' she said. (Poor darling, she had seen her mother dead, but had never had to do anything to 'lay her out', so I think she was very brave to help me.) As I turned Albion over he had a severe haemorrhage through the mouth. Poor Vera, I felt for her. It took us about an hour to do all that was necessary and it was nearly 4 o'clock. I made tea and toast and we sat quietly and companionably together. I am glad the doctor insisted on me having a friend! Mr and Mrs Wilson made all the funeral arrangements. Eustace arrived on the Monday and Albion was buried in Wick churchyard. I did not cry at all. It was not until I went the next evening and sat by his grave that the tears came.

Chapter 25

It was three months after Albion died that Harry asked me to marry him. I had no wish to ever marry him. I was not a bit in love with him, but loved him as a true friend. I did not want to hurt his feelings so I said, 'Harry, I can't. It is much too soon.'

'Well, I am sure Albion expected us to marry. He put our hands together and how can I really look after you if we don't marry,' he said.

I said, 'Ask me again in a year's time, but go on being my good friend,' which he did.

Christmas came and on Christmas Eve I was popped into hospital with tummy pains, and I had my second operation for a duodenal ulcer. (I had the first one in 1938.) I was in hospital from Christmas Eve until the middle of February, and when I came out I found that Harry was ill in bed. He died at the end of February! I was sad to lose such a wonderful friend. He had left me half the interest on his money; the other half was left to his housekeeper, Miss Richardson. I think she was very good to him and very fond of him. I am glad he had been so well cared for throughout his illness. She, poor dear, had phlebitis and could not do anything.

Albion had left very little money when he died. There was £58 in the bank and nothing more. I had the Bath house with only a mortgage of £500 with which we bought the cottage, but we owed Eustace £800 and he had asked for it soon after Albion's death. I had asked Harry's advice and he at once offered me the £800, but I was most anxious not to put myself in a position where I felt obliged to marry him. So I said, 'Thank you, but it is just your advice that I want.' So he said I would have to take up a further mortgage.

So now I had a mortgage of £1,300 and everything was going wrong in the house!

Each room had a gas meter and the people put the money in. When I got the bill from the Gas Company I would unlock each meter and was shocked to find the gas bill would be £77 and out of all five meters I would get about £42. My Albion was such a trusting man that he only had the meters locked with keys from Woolworth, so anyone could duplicate them. This they must have done, and used the same money over again, but it was never done until after Albion died. It was the same with the telephone which was in the hall with a box beside where they should pay for their calls. I paid the rent of the telephone although I had no occasion to use it. You would have thought they would have been honest enough to pay for their calls, but the telephone bill would be say (without the rent) £63 and I would take out of the box £27. I was worried to death. So unhappy without Albion and people taking advantage of me, I had the telephone taken away and I called in the gas man, and thank God I got a kind, understanding man. He said he would take out my meters and put in proper gas meters and he would run the pipes to better advantage.

I said, 'How much will all this cost?'

He said, '£47.'

I said I could not affort that and he said, 'You spend more than that each quarter paying for their gas. Besides, you can sell all your meters.' I did and they went like hot cakes. Well, he did the job and gave me a bill for only £28.

I said, 'How can this be?'

He said, 'I was able to sell some of the old piping I took out.'

I was crying with relief and he said, 'There, there. I can't bear to see anyone cheated.' How I said in my prayers that night, 'God bless him.'

I had one or two other upsets. Two men left without paying, but somehow the gas man had cheered me up so much that I seemed able to cope with things as they came. In the meantime I worked in the cottage, but not the garden, and gradually got it looking quite nice. I distempered the walls. We were rather short of furniture so I thought the first flat that comes empty I will remove all the furniture and finish furnishing the cottage, and send the rest to the auction sale-room, and this I did. The flat let for the same rent as when it was furnished and people were thankful to get flats.

Ours was a very beautiful house with wonderful views. As I got money from selling furniture I gradually had improvements made to the cottage. I had had the new staircase which was lovely, and I was able to pay for that with the money I got from a little insurance I had been paying into. I got

£118 and the new staircase cost only £21. Harry's two cousins, who were carpenters did it, and did it beautifully. I now arranged with a builder to put in main drainage and water. I called up Dr Hughes at the big house and asked if my man could dig a tunnel in his meadow and fix the pipes for the main drainage and also pipes for water. He gave his permission and said a meter could be put in as the water would come from his pipes. So all this was done and the builder asked if I would give him so much every now and again so that he could buy things he needed. This arrangement suited me. I had a gardener for two hours a week, but he had been a carpenter so I got him to make a window in the big landing, and I had partitioned off 8 ft by 8 ft and had this made into a bathroom, and the bucket privy I had made into a flush toilet. The whole works cost me under £600 which I was able to pay as I had gradually unfurnished all the flats. I had also got a man who would arrange to have the trees cut down, if the doctor would approve. The man offered the doctor £120 for the tress and he was well satisfied, and I was able to gather up clumps and chippings that kept my sitting-room fire going for many a night.

All the flats were let in the Bath house so I was able to meet my bills. I had to go to hospital and have my knee cap removed as my leg was locked. I got over that all right, but the second Christmas after Albion died I had to have an operation for a duodenal ulcer. While I was in there Harry became ill and I had only been home two weeks when he died. He had come with me when I was taken to hospital. It was Christmas Eve and he waited until I was safely in bed. It was near midnight when he started to walk home, but why did he walk? Why on earth did he not take a taxi? He said it took him nearly three hours to get home and he was exhausted. That was the start of his illness. He died in February 1956. I was very sad to lose such a loving friend.

I stayed in the cottage on my own for five years; then I thought I would sell it. The garden was big and I was no gardener. Although I had a man for a couple for hours twice a week, it was nothing like enough to keep the garden looking nice, and the gardeners I had were mad on growing vegetables, and all I wanted was flowers. So I put the cottage up for sale for £3,000. It was worth it as it now had tap water, a good bathroom with basin and lavatory, and a flush toilet in the garden.

Chapter 26

One morning I had a phone call from my brother and he said, 'Hello Jessica, I am still out of work so we thought we would go to Paris for the day and we wondered if you would like to come with us.'

I said, 'You are daft. You should be taking care of your money if you are out work! It's nice of you to ask me, but I have just put the cottage up for sale and I might have prospective buyers calling. I am sorry.'

Actually I could not leave my dear dog Jackie as I knew it would not be just one day, but three before I got home. The phone went again and it was Marjorie Naish.

'Hello Jess,' she said, 'anything interesting happening in your life?'

I said, 'No, but my brother has just offered to take me to Paris for the day, but I have had to turn it down.'

'You silly thing,' said Marjorie, 'you know I would look after Jackie. You get on the phone and ask him if the offer is still going.'

I did, and he said, 'Have you got someone to mind the dog?'

'I never mentioned the dog,' I said.

'I know you didn't, but I knew that was the difficulty. Well, be up here about tea-time on Friday and we will go to Southampton and catch the boat.'

Now I should have realised that Chris must have had an ulterior motive for asking me, as they had never done so before, and he (they) certainly had. Well, I got to London and went on the Underground at Earls Court and sat opposite a most elegant looking gentleman. I thought, 'My, I would not mind knowing him.' He alighted at Richmond and so did I. I walked behind him up the platform. He had a beautiful walk and was, I thought, 6 ft. 1 in. tall. He went up to my brother who was watiting by the car.

'Hello George,' said Chris, 'I thought my sister would be on this train. Oh, there she is,' he said, catching sight of me behind George.

Chris introduced us and George said, 'Well, I sat opposite this little lady all the way from Earls Court, and I thought how lovely she looked and how I would like to know her.'

I laughed and said, 'I thought you a most elegant gentleman and how I would like to know you.'

Chris drove us to their very nice flat in Richmond and as soon as we arrived George immediately emptied all the overflowing waste-paper baskets, which greatly impressed me! Eleanor used to boast that she was the world's worst housekeeper and she certainly was, (but I thought it nothing to boast about!) Well, we had a pleasant time in Paris; my first visit and I would have liked to have gone to interesting places, but all they did was wander round one shop after another, which I did find fascinating.

I can't remember what time we reached Southampton when we came back, but Chris said, 'As I have to take you to Wick we may as well all stay the night if that is all right by you?'

'Oh yes,' I said, 'so long as I can pick up a few necessary things here,' which I did. I bought a cooked chicken and George carved it and he was shocked to see that it was mouldy. George said he would avoid the mouldy bits and I was to say nothing. What the eye doesn't see the heart doesn't grieve over. I would have had plenty of reserve food, but as I was hoping to sell within a week or two, which I did, I had reduced my stock. Eleanor and Chris had no idea the chicken was mouldy and none of us had any ill effects from it.

The cottage did look lovely and Eleanor and George both seemed most impressed. When they left, George held my hand longer than was necessary and whispered, 'You will be hearing from me.'

George's wife was Eleanor's younger sister and she had died four years ago, so George was on the look out for a wife and one who was comfortably off. He thought I was. He was a gambler and the only money he had was his pension of £4 per week and a few pounds he earned as a sort of night porter at an hotel (but he gave up this job as soon as we married). He wrote to me and came to visit me on one or two occasions and he invited me to Bournemouth. He said he had booked me in at an hotel near to his flat. I had a pleasant weekend, but I did not go to his flat, and he left me to pay the hotel bill. When I invite friends and book them into a hotel I always pay the bill. They are my guests and if I had spare bedrooms I would, of course, put them up.

The cottage was sold and I went to stay with Marjorie Naish in Bath. George invited me again to Bournemouth, but I said I would just go for the day. Then he asked me to marry him. I was not in love with him, but I was quite charmed by him and I was lonely. So I thought I might as well. Of course I had no idea what his financial position was. I thought he must be reasonably well-to-do. He had taken me to a most expensive restaurant for dinner and he was beautifully dressed. It was only after we were married that he told me that he had borrowed £30 off my brother so as to impress me. He impressed me all right! Chris and Eleanor were sitting on the promenade and he took me to them and told them we were engaged. They were delighted and George and Chris hugged each other. Both of them had glasses in their pockets, and both of them cracked them!

We were married on 3 October 1959. I did not know until afterwards that it was the fourth anniversary of his wife's death! We had a very nice wedding at the little church at Wick and a reception afterwards at the Royal York Hotel. There were forty-two guests. George said would I mind paying for his daughter Gillian (adopted) and her seven-year-old son Ian for bed and breakfast. All George's family and Eleanor and Chris had come overnight. When Basil was given his account, George asked him if he was paying in cash and when he said he was, George asked to let him have the cash as he needed it for tips, which he did not, as I paid for the reception including tips and ended up by paying the overnight accommodation for all his family and my brothers. I was shocked when I heard Chris say, on being handed his account, 'Oh my sister will take care of that.' So I paid for ten for bed and breakfast, and the whole of the reception, including 12 bottles of champagne which I myself never tasted as I am a teetotaller.

We got to Bournemouth around tea-time and went to George's 'flat' which I found was a bed-sitting-room!

I said, 'George, is this all your flat? I can't spend our married life in a bed-sitting-room after living in a lovely cottage with eight rooms.'

He said, 'I know my dear, my love. As soon as we get back from the honeymoon you must buy a little house.'

He said he would take me out to dinner that night, but when I started to unpack a few things I found that Marjorie had filled our suitcases and even my sewing case with confetti. I could have killed her! I was miserable! I felt I had made a big mistake and what with a weekend in a bed-sit and all the confetti to clear up, I told George I was much too cross to go out. So we sat at a tiny card table and opened a tin of corn-beef which we had with bread and butter. When we got into bed George put his hand on my bare shoulder and it was very cold. I yelled, 'George, don't ever do that again! Do warm your hands before you get into bed.' Next night I waited for the touch of ice, but he had woollen gloves on! How I laughed!

We got on the boat ready for the outgoing tide around 11 o'clock and George pushed me into what I thought would be a two-berth cabin. Instead it was a six-berth and four men were already in bed.

'George,' I said, 'I can't sleep in here with these men.'

He pushed me again onto a lower berth and said, 'Lie there and shut up!'

What a honeymoon! Of course I did not take my clothes off and how I washed in the morning I can't remember. I was absolutely furious. He had asked me for £300 to pay travelling expenses and in 1959, £300 was quite a large sum. Well, we stayed in Paris for the weekend and that was very nice. He took me to the Follies Bergère which I enjoyed very much. On Sunday we went to Notre Dame and outside the Cathedral were men selling filthy postcards! On Monday we continued our journey to Nice and stayed at a very nice hotel. We were booked for full board and the first evening after we arrived George and I had dinner together. There were not many guests as it was at the end of the season.

Next afternoon George took me to a very nice café kept by two Scots ladies. 'Now, my dear my love,' he said, 'you enjoy yourself and I am going to the Casino for a while.' He did not come in for dinner, so after I had had another stroll I came in and went to bed; and that pattern went on for the whole six weeks we were in Nice. I did not like to sit down to dinner on my own as the people knew we were on our honeymon, so each afternoon I would go to the café tea-room and buy something while there for my supper. I found it very dull. I was afraid to go too far in case I got lost. My lack of French was a great drawback.

I had told George that a friend of mine had given me the address of a French lady living in Nice who had bought two of her Gavin puppies which she bred, and she had asked me if I would call on her as she said she was always anxious about the homes she sold per puppies to. She did not tell me that there was a little matter of £8 owing to her for transport. After great difficulty we found the villa and were very pleasantly entertained to tea. The lady did not speak any English but the daughter did, so I chatted to her, and George, in his excellent French, chatted to the mother. She told George about the £8 she owed and asked if we would be so kind as to pay my friend in English money if she paid us in French. George assured her it was a pleasure (you bet it was, for him!) The puppies were in a most happy home with two or three other dogs and a couple of cats! George had been worrying me for some more money to go to the Casino on this our last night, but I had said, 'No, George, I must keep enough money for the return journey.' We were breaking our journey in Paris. So when he got the equivalent of £8 in French money off he went to the Casino, and for the first time won! How much, I don't know. He did not give me one cent of it and I had to write out a cheque for £8 to pay my friend!

As soon as we got back to England I started looking for a small house and was lucky to find a very nice one with three bedrooms and a lovely garden for £3,000 which I could just afford to buy without having to take up a mortgage. I was so happy to give up cooking behind a screen on a two-burner gas ring. My furniture soon arrived from Jolly's and in no time I had the house ready, and very nice it was too. But it was quite a long way from the sea, and the tram only allowed dogs on at the conductor's discretion, and as my dear Jackie was a large collie sheep dog I did not risk going as far as the sea, but every evening I would take him for an hour or two for a walk over the Queen's golf-course. A few months after we were married my knee locked again and I was taken to hospital. I was left in a corridor for five hours lying on a stretcher bed. When eventually the doctor saw me I told him I had a locked cartilage which I had had before and, if he did not mind, I would like to be transferred to Bath Hospial where I was sure Mr Barstow would attend to me.

The next day I was sent to Bath and dear Mr Barstow undertook the operation. So again I was in hospital for six weeks. George would visit me once a week, and of course my Bath friends lost no time in coming to see me. When I got back to Bournemouth I was, of course, still in plaster and had to go from time to time to Bath Hospital as an out-patient. When I got home I found that George had taken all my wedding presents to the sale-rooms to be sold by auction! I said, 'Why, George, why?'

He said, 'We have everything we needed in the house and these were all extras.'

'But they were presents, George, and I was so pleased with all of them.'

I felt I could never forgive him, but how could he do such a thing? I had left him with money, and he had his pension, so why did he do it?

Well, in spite of this and other money trouble, George was quite nice to live with. We laughed a lot and he was kind. He noticed if I was tired and would say, 'You sit there. I will get the lunch,' and he would, and get it very nicely. Sometimes in the evening he would say, 'I will make you a nice omelette,' and he made a lovely omelette. I never told him that I did not really care for omelettes!

I took him to Canada for six months. I say I took him because I paid for everything. We went by boat, which is my favourite way of travelling. It was a freighter and there were only ten passengers. George got on well with the Captain, but then he usually got on well with everyone, except my sister Annie. She did not like him. She called him 'The Charming Parasite' and asked why need I spend time with him. I should spend more time with her. So when we got to my brother Frank in Midland, and after we had been with him for two weeks he said, 'Jess, why don't you go back to Montreal with the sergeant-major (Annie) and leave George with us. We like him and like having him, and it will stop her from grumbling!' So Annie and I went back to Montreal (St Eustace) and on the railway platform she fell over someone's suitcase and broke her arm. So instead of giving me a really nice time, which I am sure she intended doing, I had to help her dress and dress her hair, which she had never had cut, and which was still very long and beautiful. I said to her once, 'Annie, you have grown into a very lovely lady.' (She was seventy-nine.)

She said, 'I know, and I always was better looking than you'!

George came three days before we sailed home. We went on the same boat that we arrived on. The Captain seemed quite pleased to welcome us! One good thing about travelling with George, he arranged everything and did it well (except for our honeymoon).

When we got home George said, 'My dear, my love, I want you to buy me a new overcoat as I had mine stolen on Toronto Station.'

I asked, 'How did that happen?'

He said, 'I put it on top of my suitcase when I went to the information desk and when I came back my coat was gone!'

I said, 'George, how could anyone so used to travelling as you have been all your life, do such a stupid thing?'

He shut me up and I will do anything for a quiet life! When we got home I bought him not only an overcoat, but also a suit. Years later when George was dead and I was visiting Frank's widow she said, 'That George you married was a funny man.'

I said, 'Funny ha ha or funny peculiar?'

'Funny peculiar,' she said. 'While he was here he sold his overcoat, a suit, and a pair of shoes to the Harbour Master.'

I said, 'He told me he had had his overcoat stolen.'

I can't think what he did with his money. I had left enough with Frank and Cissie to pay for his food and each time he wrote to me he said, 'Send me some spondulas.' I would put in a $10 note each time. He really did cost me a fortune!

One year he said he would like to take me to Biaritz and suggested that we asked the Wilsons if they would like to join us. They were delighted and

George made all the arrangements.

When Edith said, 'Jess, I mentioned to my friend Phyl Curtis that we were going to Biaritz, and she wants to come with us.'

'Oh dear,' I said, 'George won't like that. He has made all the arrangements for just the four of us.'

He did not like it at all and made a great fuss, but altered the arrangements. This was my first meeting with Phyl and we both seemed to like each other. We stayed at a lovely hotel and except for one English lady who was a permanent guest, we were the only guests. The couple who kept the hotel had lost their money and this hotel had been their private home and was filled with lovely antique furniture. The staircase was oak and the stairs were uncarpeted. It would have been a sin to cover those lovely stairs with carpet.

It was now the second Thursday of our visit and at about eight o'clock there was a lot of running up and down stairs. I said to George, 'There must be something the matter.' Just then, Phyl and the Wilsons came into our room. Phyl was crying and she said she had heard from home that her husband was ill and she would have to go at once; would George take her to Orley Airport as she did not speak any French.

'No, I certainly won't,' said George. 'I never asked you to come in the first place, and I am not going to give up three days of my holiday for you'! I could not believe what I was hearing.

Dear Mr Wilson said, 'I would take you, Phyl, but I don't speak any French.'

So Edith said, 'I'll go with you, Phyl, I speak a little French.'

I said, 'And so do I, and I will come too. I would not stay another night with that man,' pointing my finger at George. George bought our tickets and made all arrangements.

Edith said, 'I have paid our hotel bill, and the owner was very good. He has not charged for these three days.'

'Oh my goodness,' I said, 'thank you for reminding me. I must pay our bill.'

I did and said to George, 'Everything is paid up till you leave and here is 50 francs for you.'

He said, 'Is that all you are giving me? You are mean!' And I had paid for everything for both of us!

Albany (Wilson) used to walk and find all the interesting places, and when we met at lunch he would say, 'Girls, there is a lovely cove (or spot or whatever). You must walk there. You will love it.'

George would sit outside a café near the Casino sipping an aperitif waiting for it to open. Then he would go in and stay until twelve or one o'clock, just tearing himself away to come to the hotel for dinner. I don't think he ever won anything!

The next year Edith and I went to San Sebastian for a couple of weeks. It rained nearly all the time, but we enjoyed it. I caught a wretched cold and George, in his usual fond way said, 'My dear, my love, you must go to bed and I will look after you.' That was on Saturday and I was glad to go to bed as I felt rotten.

But on Wednesday he said, 'You get up. I am going to bed; I'm ill!'

So, feeling much better, I was glad to be up and about and George got into bed.

'Send for the doctor,' he said.

'What shall I say is the matter with you?' I asked.

'Tell him I've got rheumatism.'

'George', I said, 'he won't come for rheumatism and I doubt if he will come at all as you have made me call him so many times for nothing.' I did not call him, but kept George in bed as much as I could. He was not an easy patient.

On Sunday, Edith called. 'How are you Jess?' she said. 'You were rather bad when we parted.'

'Oh, I'm fine, thank you, but George is not well. Come and say hello and have a look at him. He is in the kitchen having breakfast.'

She went in and asked George how he was and he said, 'Very bad.' He did look bad and I thought I ought to send for the doctor.

Edith said, 'Jess, he looks really ill. Have you sent for the doctor?' I said I would right away.

I said to the doctor, 'Please do come. I know I have sent for you a few times, but this time he really is ill.'

So he came and said he *was* ill. I asked him what was wrong and he said that George told him he had not passed water for five days.

'But that is ridiculous', said the doctor. 'He would be dead if he had not. I'll come again tomorrow.'

Next morning Dr Pinegar came. 'Good morning, Mr Lilof. I am glad to see you looking so well. Dr Beavis said you were very ill. You must have improved.'

I could hardly believe my ears. I thought George looked dreadfully ill. A little later in the day George had evidently tried to get to the bathroom. I found him lying in the hall in a pool of water. It was like the river Avon! Had his bladder burst? I got him up with great difficulty; he was a tall man 6 ft. 1 in. and I am 5 ft. 2in. He was holding onto the bannister and as fast as I released one hand he would grab with the other. Eventually I got him into the bathroom (on the same floor), sponged him down and put him on clean pyjamas, and he walked back into bed. I could see he was dying. So I phoned Dr Beavis and he said he would come, but George passed away before he arrived. I told him about the flooding, but he did not take much notice.

I said, 'What are you going to put on the death certificate?'

He said, 'Pneumonia.'

He is buried in Lansdown Cemetery and all his family came. I missed him, but his loss was not like the loss of Albion whom I miss every day.

Chapter 27

Four years after George died, my nephew Jim came over from Quebec with his wife to visit me. It was the first time I had met Peggy and she seemed quite charming. She was very impressed with my house and could not help saying, 'Aunt Jessica, what a beautiful house this is!'

'Yes, it is, but I am now eighty-four and I think the time has come for me to sell it!'

That was all I said, but when they got back to Quebec Peggy wrote and said that she would like to buy the house! I asked £7,500 for it in 1971. When she sold it in 1984 she got over £200,000.

In due course Peggy arrived and was my guest for a month so that I could show her how I ran the house. I had the hall floor flat and the other four were let to very nice tenants. We had Mrs Elliot in the top flat and she had worked for me and for two of the other flat tenants for over twenty years. Among her jobs were the seventy-nine stairs, hall and three large landings which she cleaned each week. None of us had ever had any cause to be in any way displeased with her, but after I left and moved into a flat in St James's Square, Peggy accused Mrs Elliot of stealing an electric fire and made her life so miserable that she was forced to move out and stop working for Mr Askew and Miss P.

Then she had lots of quarrels with Mrs Ramsey in the garden flat. I had told Peggy that Mrs Ramsey was the best tenant I had ever had! So Mrs Ramsey moved out. Peggy now had two empty flats and somehow she did not seem content to settle on the hall floor. For a time she moved to the top of the house in Mrs Elliot's flat where she stayed for a few months. Then she moved down into the garden flat. What a restless unpredictable person she was turning out to be. As soon as the hall floor flat was vacant Mr Askew asked if he and his wife Norah could move into it, as he was finding the stairs rather trying. So Peggy allowed him to, and then she came to me and begged me to go and live in my old home. 'Please come, Aunt Jess. I would so love to have you in the house and you have always wanted the drawing-room flat.' This was quite true, but it had never been vacant. Well, although I was distressed to know about Peggy's treatment of Mrs Elliot and Mrs Ramsay, I thought she would be all right with me, because I never quarrelled with anyone!

I had the flat redecorated, which cost me nearly £1,000. I was so pleased with it and for a time, in fact several months, all was well. I thought I would go to Canada for a month. I booked my berth on a Russian ship; the fare to Montreal was £104. Then six weeks before I was due to travel (in September) I had news from one of my nieces to say that my sister had died. She was ninety-four years old and I think had been failing for several months. So I went to the travel agents and explained the situation and they refunded my money, all except £10, which I thought was very fair of them. At this time I had my nephew staying with me. That is to say he came to me each day for meals, but was obliged to sleep out as I had only one bedroom. He was planning to return home and asked me to go with him. 'You have never met any of my family, Aunt Jess, and I would like you to get to know them. You could use the money you were going to use to go to Canada.'

So it was arranged. My friend, Mrs Wilson, said she would go in and water my plants and feed the birds on the balcony. I had a very nice quite uneventful time in Pasadena, and was pleased to make the acquaintance of David's family.

When we got back in a month's time, Mrs Wilson met us at the station with a most unhappy expression.

'Whatever has happened, Edith?' I asked. 'Has Albany died?'

'No', she said, 'but Peggy is behaving in a most peculiar way and has upset me very much.'

She said when she went in to water the plants Peggy met her in the hall and said, 'Who let you into my house and what are you doing in my house?' Edith explained that I had given her keys and that she had come to water the plants and feed the birds.

The next time Edith came she could not get in with the front door key so rang the bell. When Peggy let her in she gave Edith a letter which read: 'Dear Edith, If you must come to my house, come at a time to suit me, after 5.30. (It was January and Edith at the other side of Bath.) Someone will let you in and will wait and see you out.'

Edith was very upset over this letter and took it to my solicitor, and that was the start of the most unhappy year of my life.

When I saw Peggy she held up a key and said, 'Here is the key to the front door of my house, and kindly see that no one uses it except a tenant living in my house.'

Peggy used to leave notes on the hall table; anyone could read them! One read: 'Mrs Godwin, you old bitch, I see you are still feeding the pigeons to the detriment of *my property*.' I did not feed the pigeons, I had a flat wooden box on the balcony and in this I would put bread crumbs chopped up, bacon rinds and any other bits. I had sparrows, robins, and chaffinches. I also hung up bags of peanuts for the blue tits; very occasionally a couple of pigeons would come.

Three weeks later Peggy gave me four weeks notice to leave! She could not get me out, but she was being so unpleasant in dozens of little ways that I lost no time in hunting for an unfurnished flat. Edith's daughter-in-law, Sue, would drive us round to look at places and how awful some of them were. I was in despair. What with the miserable atmosphere at 35 Belvedere, and the seeming hopelessness of finding a flat, I got very low. I was 89 years old. Then in answer to prayer, Sue heard of this flat and knew Mr Moore who was the owner and who was converting this lovely Georgian house into five flats. She took me to see him and he let me have it 'for my life'. I was willing to buy it, but for reasons known to himself he did not want to sell it. I paid him £8,500 and here I am, 99 years old and still here. When I unexpectedly saw Mr Moore, the first thing I said was, 'Oh Mr Moore, I do apologise for living so long.'

He laughed and said, 'Mrs Godwin, if you are as happy as you seem to be and are so well loved, you are welcome to stay in my flat for another ten or twenty years!'

I told Peggy when I would be leaving and found another note on the table: 'Mrs Godwin. I have arranged to have a man to take down the curtains in your flat, as I want to be sure I have the antique curtain rods, knowing I cannot trust you!' Well! My nephew, her husband, had only paid me £7,500 for the whole fifteen roomed house, and that did not include my furniture. When Peggy sold the house a few years later, she got over £200,000 for it.

I could not have the bedroom without curtains on the windows, which were only 12 inches from the floor and were in full view of people in the street and the people across the road. I got in touch with my solicitor and he said she had no right to do that and she had to get the curtains hung up again. She continued to harass me. When I put my rent on the table, which was what we all did with our rent books, she would leave mine with a note 'Not acceptable'. At the end of another note she left for me she put, 'Do take this to your solicitor and let him see how I am harassing you, you old Bitch!'

Oh well, I am glad I never see her now, neither does Jim, my nephew (and her ex-husband), but he hears news of her sometimes from his grown-up children. We think she is living in a sheltered home in Scotland, but she must be a very unhappy woman. She seemed to fall out with everyone with whom she came in contact.

Chapter 28

Referring to the Goultons

I have, in my memoirs, made one or two references to my mother's gentility, so I would like to tell you a little about her background. Her parents were by birth and education, gentlefolk. Her father was a wealthy landowner. He cultivated flax and used to engage a hundred or more women from Ireland to do what has to be done to flax, about which I know nothing. I have been told that he had written and had printed a book/leaflet? about flax. He also owned a coal-mine.

Before he was married he lived at Staynor Hall which my great-grandfather rented, but when my grandfather married he bought Flaxby Lodge, also in Selby.

My Grandmother had twelve children: three died in infancy and my Uncle Robert in his teens and she, poor darling, died at the age of forty-six. The children were all educated at home, the two boys with a tutor and the girls with a governess. My mother was the third girl. There was Mary, Alice, Sarah, Annie, Alma and later a stepsister Madge. They were taught all the usual things for Victorian young ladies.

My mother spoke beautifully and had innate politeness and was recognised all her life, no matter how poorly dressed she was, or how menial the task she was doing, as a gentlewoman.

When my mother was about twenty-three years old my grandfather lost a great deal of money. Unfortunately I was never a very curious child, so I did not ask many questions about my mother's early life so I don't know how, or why grandfather lost his money. I seem to remember hearing that the coal-mine was flooded, but I am very ignorant about all these things. I know my mother was engaged to a young gentleman who had eleven sisters. He was the only boy and he jilted my mother. He said he was very sorry, but he *had* to marry a girl with money as he would have to support any of his sisters who did not marry. I do remember asking my mother if she was very upset and she said, 'My dear, I think it broke my heart!'

My Uncle William was engaged to an Earl's daughter. It could well have been the Earl of Yarborough's daughter as the two families were on very friendly terms. The Earl must have been very friendly with my great-uncle Richard as he had an urn erected in his memory in Brocklesby Park. On the inscription it says:

> The Earl of Yarborough
> Dedicates this urn to the memory
> of Richard Goulton of Bonby
> A tenant and friend who in grateful respect
> Bequeathed a legacy to his Lordship.

Well, owing to the reduced circumstances of my grandfather, the Earl would not allow my Uncle William to marry his daughter. My Uncle was very angry and said he would marry the first girl he met. When he reached home there was this new governess engaged to teach the two youngest girls, Alma and Madge (so he could not have been really poor!) Her name was Helen Jackson, and her father was Governor of Norwich Prison for twenty-six years. My Uncle William fell in love with her (she was very pretty) and they were married. But it seems to have been kept secret because six months later Uncle James asked her to marry him and she said, 'I'm sorry James, but I am already married to William.' James was furious with William and he left the house, and the brothers never spoke to each other again although they both lived to be over eighty.

It was now decided that the four elder girls would have to earn their own living and they were sent to a training college for young ladies, at Zeals, but I cannot find this place on the map. I have an old letter of my mother's in which she says it was quite a little village, a few miles from Bath – a Church of England college and High Church at that! Just fancy, it is about 120 years ago since my mother was there! Mary, the eldest girl, became a governess and got a job in Paris in a Count's family which she kept for four years. She then married her sweetheart who had been waiting for her for several years. He, Charles Drake, was a wealthy farmer in Dorset and alas, he let my grandfather have his farm as a security on some of his speculations and lost everything, which caused my uncle to have to emigrate to Canada and take a plot of 125 acres, which was given to any farmer who would clear the land and work it. What a hard life it must have been to my uncle who had been brought up as a gentleman farmer, and hard for my aunt to struggle in a primitive kitchen after living in Paris in a Count's family. But they were young and in love, and my aunt said that Uncle Charles *never* once reminded her that it was through her father they were in that position.

My Aunt Grace decided to become a missionary and went to South Africa taking my Aunt Alice with her. Of course, I never ever met either of them as they never returned to England.

My mother did not like children so did not become a governess, and she did not want to be a lady's companion, but she found she did enjoy cooking; so she came to Worthing and got a position as cook, which did not go down at all well with her family. In fact she became estranged from them. At Worthing she met my father who was a master baker and a widower with a grown-up married family. He fell deeply in love with my mother who at that time must have been lonely and unhappy. She married my father who was thirty years her senior and I've heard was happy with him. They had seven children, but he died when I was three years old and my brother Willie two days. But I have told of this at the beginning of my memoirs.

I never knew what my uncles did for a living. I had met my Uncle William a couple of times and liked him very much. He was 'something in the City' (London). My mother said he speculated, but whatever he did, they were *very* comfortably off. They lived in London and in addition to taking my brother Frank when my father died, they kept my grandfather until he died at the age of eighty-eight and took him up to Selby to bury him. In Selby Abbey there is a beautiful stained glass window to the memory of my grandmother's father, James Banks of Wiston Manor.

I fear my mother was a great disappointment to her family: first in choosing a menial occupation and then to marry into 'trade'. But I think as time went by they recognised my father as a lovely man. But when after being a widow for five years, she married my stepfather, Jim Tribe, an ignorant, uneducated and bone lazy man, they certainly had good cause to absolutely ignore her which is what they did, with the exception of Uncle William, her eldest brother, who used to pop over from London to Brighton to spend half a day with her. I used not to see him. My mother would meet him at the station and my job was to keep my stepfather out of the way. Uncle did not come to the house, but my mother would meet him at the station, and he would take her somewhere for a meal; then I suppose just sit on the sea front and chat. But what a treat for mother!

I once asked her why she married Jim Tribe and she said he showed her his rent book to prove he paid his way, and he said he would be happy to make a home for her and my brother William. She was lonely and at a difficult age and also suffered from migraine so I suppose she thought it would be security. But instead of having just Willie to keep, she also had Jim Tribe and me. Ah well, she spent the last thirty-six years of her life in Canada, where for a short time she had her three grown-up sons with her and my sister Annie. She was reconciled to her sister Mary, and met her youngest sister Alma married to a vicar. (They had six daughters!)

My mother died peacefully at the age of ninety-four. As Queen Catharine said of Wolsey (to paraphrase): So may she rest. Her faults lie gently on her!

Green Park, Bath

Green Park, Bath